NEW DIRECTIONS FOR ADULT AND CONTINUING EDUCATION

Ralph G. Brockett, *University of Tennessee, Knoxville*
Susan Imel, *Ohio State University*
EDITORS-IN-CHIEF

Alan B. Knox, *University of Wisconsin, Madison*
CONSULTING EDITOR

Workplace Learning

W. Franklin Spikes
Kansas State University

EDITOR

Number 68, Winter 1995

JOSSEY-BASS PUBLISHERS
San Francisco

WORKPLACE LEARNING
W. Franklin Spikes (ed.)
New Directions for Adult and Continuing Education, no. 68
Ralph G. Brockett, Susan Imel, Editors-in-Chief
Alan B. Knox, Consulting Editor

ISSN 0195-2242   ISBN 0-7879-9937-7

NEW DIRECTIONS FOR ADULT AND CONTINUING EDUCATION is part of The
Jossey-Bass Higher and Adult Education Series and is published quarterly
by Jossey-Bass Inc., Publishers, 350 Sansome Street, San Francisco,
California 94104-1342. Second-class postage paid at San Francisco,
California, and at additional mailing offices. POSTMASTER: Send address
changes to New Directions for Adult and Continuing Education, Jossey-
Bass Inc., Publishers, 350 Sansome Street, San Francisco, California
94104-1342.

SUBSCRIPTIONS for 1995 cost $48.00 for individuals and $64.00 for institutions, agencies, and libraries.

EDITORIAL CORRESPONDENCE should be sent to the Editor-in-Chief, Susan
Imel, ERIC/ACVE, 1900 Kenny Road, Columbus Ohio 43210-1090.
E-mail: imel.1@osu.edu.

Cover photograph by Wernher Krutein/PHOTOVAULT © 1990.

TCF Manufactured in the United States of America on Lyons Falls
Pathfinder Tradebook. This paper is acid-free and 100 percent
totally chlorine-free.

CONTENTS

EDITOR'S NOTES

The evidence is clear. More and more adults are engaged in workplace-based learning activities than ever before. Workplace learning is a multibillion-dollar enterprise in which employees learn new skills designed to help them keep their organizations competitive in an increasingly global economic environment. Carnevale and Carnevale (1994) indicate that formal corporate training initiates have increased 45 percent between 1983 and 1991. More current data support the continuing increase in expenditures and participation in workplace learning programs. By some estimates, enrollment in workplace learning programs annually exceeds the total enrollment in the nation's 3,300 colleges and universities.

With the increase in workplace learning activities has come a change in the perceived role and function of training and workplace units. The old adage of trainers being the last hired and first fired no longer holds. Learning in the workplace is now viewed by most modern, globally competitive organizations as a key strategy in achieving core business objectives. Now viewed as a central rather than tangential business function, workplace learning programs reach all levels of employees, from the shop floor to the executive boardroom. Ranging from basic and functional literacy skills to high technology and sophisticated management practices, workplace education is playing a pivotal role in transforming traditional employer and employee relationships, business practices, and organizations into today's reengineered, team-oriented, learning-oriented entities.

This issue of *New Directions in Adult and Continuing Education* is designed to address some of the more interesting and critical workplace education issues. Karen Watkins sets the stage for this discussion in Chapter One, where she describes the historical evolution of the field of workplace learning, provides some definitions of commonly used terminology, and identifies issues germane to workplace learning practice. Joan Wills then examines the concept of workforce development from a policy perspective in Chapter Two. In Chapter Three, Joan Schwartz and E. Nelson Swinerton of the American Council on Education discuss workplace learning and explain how such programs are being linked to college and university academic credit. In Chapter Four, Iris Saltiel looks at experiential learning in the workplace from a broad perspective and ties together how colleges and universities have worked together in academic partnership arrangements to advance employee educational programs. In Chapter Five, I discuss the preparation of workplace learning professionals. In Chapter Six, Sue Folinsbee discusses the need to rethink the professional preparation of workplace educators along with a lifelong career development model. In Chapter Seven, Gene Roth describes how advances in technology have affected today's workplace learning initiatives. In Chapter

Eight, I focus on future issues in the delivery, management, and evaluation of workplace learning programs.

The workplace of yesterday is very different from today's and will be almost unrecognizable by the workers of tomorrow. Consequently, workplace educators will remain on the front end of organizational change and advancement. It is for this important group of adult educators that this volume has been written. We hope it will serve as an impetus for ongoing discussion about workplace learning and the improvement of day-to-day workplace learning practice.

W. Franklin Spikes
Editor

Reference

Carnevale, A. P., and Carnevale, E. S. "Growth Patterns in Workplace Training." *Training and Development,* May 1994, pp. 22–28.

W. FRANKLIN SPIKES *is professor, Department of Foundations and Adult Education, Kansas State University.*

This chapter offers a brief history of the field, a portrait of workplace learning today, contrasting definitions, and emerging issues that are changing workplace learning practices.

Workplace Learning: Changing Times, Changing Practices

Karen E. Watkins

Learning in the workplace is a relatively recent phenomenon. On the other hand, it is the largest adult education endeavor. Like the workplace that forms its context, learning in the workplace is experiencing high-speed, exponentially escalating changes. This chapter is not an exhaustive look at past, present, and future, but rather a glimpse at the factors that appear to significantly influence the future of workplace learning.

Workplace learning encompasses several other terms including *training* and *human resource development*. These terms will be used somewhat interchangeably in this chapter, but a distinction at the outset is in order. Initially, *training* was the prevalent term, and it appropriately referred to job-related instruction. Later, *human resource development* was coined by Leonard Nadler (Nadler and Nadler, 1989) to mean all those activities that developed people as resources for organizations. Performance technologists prefer the term *human performance technology,* which emphasizes strategies to engineer performance, including changes in work processes and other organizational systems that affect human performance (Swanson and Torraco, 1995). *Workplace learning* encompasses what learners do rather than focusing solely on what trainers or developers do in organizations. As this chapter illustrates, the increasing demand for learning at work coupled with an emphasis on more informal, self-directed learning practices makes *workplace learning* a helpful semantic differentiation. This evolving terminology mirrors both the history of the field and the continuing tensions between individual and organizational emphases, between learning and performance.

New Directions for Adult and Continuing Education, no. 68, Winter 1995   © Jossey-Bass Publishers

Changing Times: A Brief History of Workplace Learning

While some argue that training can be traced back to early cave paintings that depicted hunting lessons, most formal interest in training as a field dates back to the early 1900s. At the beginning of the industrial revolution, in the 1700s, apprenticeships in crafts were common means to attain more advanced skills, but conditions were often difficult. There was little or no attempt, other than that by the craft guilds, or what we would now think of as trade unions, to set standards for apprenticeships. During the 1800s, corporations such as the Lowell textile mills in Lowell, Massachusetts, began to show an early interest in worker education, focusing more on education to encourage women housed in corporate boarding homes to use their leisure time constructively, within the boundaries of turn-of-the-century morality. Corporation or factory schools were the first formal programs of instruction in the workplace; R. Hoe and Company of New York City is said to have opened the first such school, one for machinists, in 1872. Railroad companies began to create these schools in the early 1900s, followed shortly by Westinghouse, Baldwin Locomotive, General Electric, International Harvester, Ford, Goodyear, and National Cash Register (Swanson and Torraco, 1995).

Improving workplace practices through performance engineering was the approach of Frederick Taylor and Lillian and Frank Gilbreth, who together conducted time and motion studies to determine the "one best way" to perform rote tasks in the early 1900s. Their goals were to improve efficiency and to reduce worker strain. Like the industrial revolution itself, with the move from holistic to specialized assembly-line work, Taylorism taught principles of scientific management, which emphasized making human work processes more scientific and machinelike.

A forgotten voice in the history of human resource development was that of Lillian Evelyn Moller Gilbreth (1878–1972), who was awarded the Hover Medal for her contributions to motion study and her integration of management engineering and human relations (Hicks, 1991). Early on, Gilbreth saw that improvements in work processes were dependent on the improvement and development of people. Together Lillian and Frank moved from construction into consulting, but Frank died unexpectedly. To keep her family of eleven children together and cared for, Lillian built a consulting business and conducted management schools in her home. "She had a great capacity for understanding and winning co-operation from workers of all varieties" (Yost, 1949, p. 330). According to Gilbreth, the aim in teaching was to train all of the senses possible, so she used a variety of instructional strategies: written, oral, and object-lesson. She believed that viewing the overall system helped the individual worker to have a grasp of the whole. These are the hallmarks of both early and present approaches to job instruction training. Her contributions extended into the 1960s as she continued to give management seminars into the later part of her long life.

In 1924, Joseph M. Juran began the work that would lead to the total quality management movement, first in Japan in the 1950s and then in the United

States in the 1980s. The introduction of total quality management principles has helped transform human resource development into a function that is more closely aligned with strategic business purposes and organizational development.

Other major impetuses for formalizing the study and practice of workplace education beyond Taylorism and the principles of scientific management were the first and second world wars. Early in the First World War, vocational educators moved to industry to help train defense industry workers. In 1906 the National Society for the Promotion of Industrial Education was formed. Systematic instructional methods were developed, and in 1917 Charles R. Allen introduced the "show, tell, do, check" method of on-the-job training to train fifty thousand shipyard workers ("The Coming of Age of Workplace Learning," 1994). Supervisors had pocket cards reminding them to tell the workers what to do, show them how to do it, have them do it, and then check to see that they understood. This method is still used in on-the-job training programs.

With the Great Depression, in the 1930s, educators became involved in training to support FDR's Civilian Conservation Corps (CCC) and other programs developed to employ workers. Primarily using vocational educators but also using engineers and other specialists, these programs trained the unemployed. The CCC, established in 1933 as a New Deal program, enlisted unemployed, unmarried young men to work on conservation and resource-development projects such as soil conservation, flood control, and protection of forests and wildlife. Enrollees were provided with food, lodging, and other necessities and were given a small monthly salary. In 1935, 2,600 CCC camps had an enrollment of five hundred thousand. The CCC was abolished in 1942. President Clinton's education program for 1995 suggests a similar program primarily directed toward unemployed youth.

In 1938 Roosevelt signed an executive order to establish a training program for White House staff. This legislation and Roosevelt's responses to the Depression initiated the role that government plays in training today. Government agencies train their staff, support training grants for government-related spending such as defense contracts, and fund training for the unemployed. Worker training legislation such as the Comprehensive Employment Training Act and subsequently the Jobs Training Partnership Act supports training of youth, displaced homemakers, and laid-off or unemployed workers.

Rosie the Riveter posters commemorate the preponderance of women and nontraditional workers in the workforce during the Second World War. Vocational educators were again asked to come to the workplace and teach masses of workers how to operate the machines of the defense industry. In 1940 the first train-the-trainer programs were established through the Training Within Industry Service of the War Manpower Commission. These were known as "J" programs and covered training in job instruction, job relations, job methods, and job safety. Designed to use simple key words to communicate ideas, the program emphasized focusing not on a training problem, but rather on production problems. This focus on learning to solve work-related problems was lost and has only recently reemerged (Swanson and Torraco, 1995).

In 1942 the American Society of Training Directors was created with fifteen training directors. Initially aimed toward the needs of training directors, it came to encompass trainers as well and was later renamed the American Society for Training and Development (ASTD) to reflect this enlarged focus. The organization grew from its initial 15 members to over 29,600 members as of 1996, and it is now the largest association for people in the training or human resource development field.

A brief chronology of changes in the field of human resource development since this time illustrates why the field has grown so quickly. In the 1960s organizational development began to flourish as an approach to work going beyond the individual to the group and intergroup issues affecting organizations. Focusing on small-group development, survey feedback, and action research approaches, these interventions moved from training people in new skills to changing groups and organizations.

In the 1970s the workplace was affected by the growing power of minority groups, civil rights and affirmative action legislation, and the influx of a more diverse workforce. Training adapted, beginning to incorporate human relations training, employee assistance programs, and career development programs designed to give employees greater control over their career mobility.

With the enormous strides in technology made in the 1980s, training began to incorporate more of the work of instructional technologists. Multimedia programs replaced programmed instruction, and training technologies moved from serving as an instructional aid to replacing traditional training methods. Distance learning strategies created new training capabilities.

By the 1990s the spate of mergers and acquisitions has led to a globalization of the workforce that has again changed the face of training. Increasing reliance on a temporary, ad hoc workforce has led to differentiated systems for delivering training, including management consultants; internal company trainers; external training agencies such as training companies, community colleges, union schools, and training centers; and multimedia companies specializing in training courses on video, on CD-ROM, or in print. Partnerships between colleges and businesses, between public schools and businesses, and between businesses to provide training are growing.

Portrait of Workplace Learning Now

The Lakewood Research Group annually surveys training directors to describe the nature of training. While its sample primarily describes training in large organizations, its training expenditure figure gives some idea of the scope of training in business and industry, since large organizations are much more likely to have formal in-house training programs. In 1995 it reported expenditures of $52.2 billion for training. This figure represents an estimated 1.59 billion hours of training for 49.6 million people. Lakewood found that expenditures for outside sources of training, such as payment for employees to attend seminars or for packaged training programs, increased by 4 percent between

1994 and 1995 to $10.3 billion, or 20 percent of total training expenditures. The largest proportion of the training budget is that for training staff salaries, now 72 percent of the total budget. Twenty-five percent of organizations say they are increasing their use of "outsourcing" as a business strategy.

Carnevale, Gainer, and Villet (1991) estimate that these figures are low if you count the real business dollars spent in more informal training such as on-the-job training or self-directed learning. Incorporating these figures suggests that costs were closer to $210 billion per year in 1988. In the same year formal education spent $238 billion (with $94 billion of that in higher education). This estimate would put workplace learning expenditures almost equal to those for all formal education.

However one counts dollars spent on work-related learning, there is little doubt that it is a massive industry. There are so many different types of workplace learning—the work of consultants, tuition reimbursement programs, in-house training programs, external continuing education programs, self-directed learning programs, quality teams, study teams, and more—that the amount spent both on the providers of this education and on the worker for time spent learning is staggering. A related problem, given the complexity of forms of workplace learning and the growing number of types of providers, is how to determine who is doing the training.

Who Trains?

According to 1983 data cited in Rothwell and Kazanas (1994), an estimated 250,000 people work full-time and another 700,000 work part-time as human resource development practitioners. But few estimates take into account all types of providers, so this figure may well be incomplete. Because of the diffuse types of providers, it is almost impossible to track how many people make their living in the human resource field. Individual consultants, large consulting firms such as Arthur Andersen, software and packaged training providers, graphics firms, divisions within other industries such as the business and industry continuing education programs of various colleges, government sponsored training programs such as the Job Training Partnership Act and workforce literacy grants, and many others make up the outsource training vendor community. Added to this is the fact that human resource development functions are so decentralized and occur under so many different titles that an organization may be unable to tell you how many people are full- or part-time human resource development practitioners within the organization. One organization I studied conducted an internal audit and came up with more than eighty people with direct or indirect connection to the education and training function. Many organizations are now using managers and other nontrainers to provide training. In 1988 over fifty corporations offered college degrees and had corporate universities; the trend continues. Little wonder that estimates of the number of people involved in the field are so difficult to make.

With such confusion about its definition, what belongs under the human resource development umbrella is also difficult to determine. When ASTD identified eleven human resource roles in 1993 (McLagan, 1993), it claimed three for human resource development: training, career development, and organization development. Yet, reality is seldom this neat. Actual titles for human resource development practitioners vary enormously, and job responsibilities are more often combinations of one or more of these three roles with other personnel roles, such as organization designer, personnel specialist, and employee assistance counselor.

Defining Human Resource Development

As the field of workplace learning has grown, definitions have evolved. Early distinctions between education and training emphasized the idea that education was more long-term and equipped an individual with lifelong attributes whereas training was for immediate job performance or vocational needs. "Education is for the rounding-out of the individual and the good of society; it is general, provides background and increases understanding. Training is for the good of plant production—it is a way to solve production problems through people; it is specific and helps people to acquire skill through the use of what they learned" (Swanson and Torraco, 1995, p. 2). Nadler and Nadler (1989) define human resource development as organized learning experiences provided by employers within a specified period of time to bring about performance improvement or personal growth. They differentiate between training that is focused on one's present job performance, education for a future job, and development that is not job-focused. Philosophically, education might be more developmental or classical whereas training is more behavioristic. These distinctions are also eroding.

With workplace learning moving toward continuous improvement at individual, team, and organizational levels (Watkins and Marsick, 1993), it is clear that a longer time perspective is needed. The dawning acknowledgment that organizational changes of processes, culture, or structure create accompanying learning demands has meant that the field of human resource development must encompass more than training (Watkins and Marsick, 1993). A number of recent definitions illustrate this broadening conception of human resource development. For example, Watkins (1989) defines human resource development as the field of study and practice responsible for fostering a long term work-related learning capacity at the individual, group, and organizational levels. This means that it includes, but is not limited to, training, career development, and organizational development. For McLagan (1993), human resource development is the improvement of individual, group, and organizational effectiveness through the integrated use of career development, organizational development, and training and development. According to Carnevale, Gainer, and Villet (1990), "The employer's goal in providing workplace learning opportunities is to improve the company's competitive advantage. Learning is linked to the bottom line." Finally, according to Goldstein (1986), "Training is the systematic acquisition of skills, rules, concepts or attitudes that result in improved performance in another environment."

Workplace learning is qualitatively different from learning in school. Resnick (1987) notes that learning outside school has five unique features: it is focused more on acquiring specific competencies than on acquiring generalized skills; more on the social than on the individual, with an emphasis on shared cognition; more on contextualized reasoning than on symbol manipulation; and more on tool manipulation than on thought activities; and it is focused on the ability to see how the whole system works.

Elsewhere (Watkins, 1991), I identified ten principles for workplace learning that emerge from these differences. They included the following: the facilitator of workplace learning must be able to use group or team learning strategies to explore and enhance socially determined learning; bring learners' implicit frames of reference to the surface; collaboratively design learning as an interactive, dialogic process; use bridging apprenticeships and coaching and case study analysis strategies to enhance transfer of learning; focus on long term strategies that make learning continuous and enhance the individual's, the group's, and the organization's learning capacities.

Workplace Learning as a Source of Growth

According to Carnevale, Gainer, and Villet (1990), econometric models show that formal education accounts for a 15 percent variation in lifetime earnings while workplace learning accounts for an 85 percent variation in lifetime earnings. Since before the Great Depression, human factors have been the major source of growth. While many have argued that the availability of labor and technology account for growth, these authors contend that it is their integration into the workforce that actually accounts for growth. We need trained labor and people who can use technology to improve overall performance.

This learning-based economic engine will need more and more fuel. It is estimated that over 75 percent of all workers will need retraining by the year 2000. With a shorter and shorter knowledge half-life (the time from entrance into the workforce until one's knowledge becomes obsolete, which in technology-intensive fields is now less than four years; see Swanson and Torraco, 1995), many workers will need to be retrained again and again. Skills needed for the new workplace are information and cognitive skills. These will also demand both different workplace learning approaches and a more constant stream of educational experiences.

Emerging Issues and Changing Practices

In an era of almost dizzying change, it is difficult to identify where a field is heading. In this section a number of the most salient trends are discussed: professionalization, increasing litigation, diffusion, new rules, technology, globalization, and reengineering.

Professionalization. As the field has grown, perhaps no issue has become more important than professionalization. The enlarged scope of the field has signaled an increased need to certify that the training and consulting being offered is reliable. Academic programs in training and human resource development have proliferated in education, business, and psychology. Certification programs in human resource development abound, as do train-the-trainer workshops. The ASTD has set competency standards for the field (McLagan, 1993). Some consultants are guaranteeing business or performance results for their efforts.

Although these efforts to guarantee competence are important first steps, they are frustrated by the lack of a common body of knowledge and by the broad scope of practice. Large corporations hire multiple expertise: organization development specialists, trainers, instructional designers, graphic artists, media specialists, management consultants, technical experts, and others. Many small companies hope to find an individual who can wear all these hats for their human resource function and more. They often also expect that the individual will handle personnel selection, compensation, and benefits. Incredibly, individuals often do just that.

A field so broad is not likely to be represented by one academic discipline, and human resource development is not. Academic preparation programs in human resource management, industrial and organizational psychology, adult education, instructional technology, vocational education, and organizational psychology offer degrees in human resource development.

Without a direct means to influence professionalization of the field, such as licensure, a number of indirect means have been employed. College degrees and certificate programs, performance-based contracting, and outsourcing training are means to control the professional competence of workplace educators. In addition, professional organizations play a role by establishing standards and creating peer networks that influence members toward these standards.

In the field of workplace learning, numerous professional organizations are involved. Organizations besides the ASTD whose members are in the training field are the Society for Human Resource Management, essentially aimed toward those who handle the personnel functions of organizations; the Society for Industrial and Organizational Psychology, with members in training and industrial assessment; and the Academy of Management, with members whose interests span human resource management, management development, and organizational development. Other human resource development practitioners are found in the International Association for Organizational Communication and in the Organization Development Network. In 1992 a group of academics with an interest in scholarship in training and development formed the Academy of Human Resource Development. The major training membership association remains the ASTD. It is in the process of redefining its mission to be more consistent with a second major training association, the National Society for Performance and Instruction. These diverse associations hint at the breadth of the field and the large number of disciplines that now have a stake in this profession. On the one hand, this might attest to one strength of the field. On the other, it suggests one reason why it has been so difficult to professionalize practice.

Increasing Litigation. When these methods of credentialing fail, legal strategies are employed. An interesting and growing body of literature identifies legal issues in training (Turner, 1995). McLagan (1993) identified a code of ethical standards as part of the Models for Excellence study. These guidelines help trainers clarify best practice, but legal precedent is increasingly mandating best practice. Contract violations such as when a vendor fails to perform to standard are generally settled out of court or in a lawsuit for the award of damages. Violations of copyright laws among trainers have led to stricter company policies and practices and therefore fewer violations. These too are seldom settled in court. As a result, the more well-known cases where legal precedent has been established have been in the areas of employee rights and safety.

The "guru training case" as it has been described in the literature actually refers to a number of cases in which employees charged that a mandatory training program violated their religious freedom. The Equal Employment Opportunity Commission issued a memorandum stating that training programs that employees felt asked them to surrender a fundamental religious belief were actionable (Eyres and Moreland, 1994). It stated that the company had an obligation to either eliminate the training or offer alternative training that would still guarantee the employees' potential upward mobility in the organization without violating their religious beliefs.

Charges of disparate treatment on the part of those providing the training illustrate another form of discrimination. A black female police recruit charged that she was judged by a different standard than were others when she flunked a firearms qualification test. Other cases attempt to establish that those responsible for on-the-job training have provided inadequate training and that this lack of training is based on race or gender. When individuals are fired for poor job performance, management may be liable if it does not have a system for ensuring that supervisors are offering on the job training and that this training is both successful and nondiscriminatory.

Selection for training also comes under scrutiny. For example, refusing to select a female employee for advanced training because she might take a maternity leave is clearly unlawful (Eyres and Moreland, 1994). The touchstone in determining whether or not discrimination has occurred is whether or not the selection procedures or criteria adversely affect one group of people. The courts have upheld such criteria as job-related experience, skills, productivity, absenteeism and tardiness, and disciplinary records.

The content of training materials must also be free of language that is discriminatory or actionable on the basis of race, age, gender, religion, national origin, or disability. This extends to video or photographic material as well.

Health and safety concerns constitute a major area of litigation. Cases of failure to train, failure to warn, and inadequate training have set standards for trainers. When a janitor in Miami inadvertently jabbed himself with an AIDS-infected needle, he sued on the grounds that he had not been trained in the proper disposal of such waste. Subsequently, OSHA changed the regulation to ensure that employees with less direct responsibility for handling these materials would be covered by the current mandatory training regulations. Failure-to-warn cases involve the charge that the training fails to warn an employee of potential danger. A truck driver died after inhaling hydrogen sulfide, and his family sued, saying that he had not been warned of the dangers. In this instance, training had occurred. The training must also be adequate. More and more, trainers are being asked not only to certify that individuals have attended such OSHA-mandated training, but also to verify that they were able to pass knowledge or performance tests. The most well-known case involving inadequate training is the *Canton, Ohio* vs. *Harris* suit decided by the Supreme Court in 1989. In this case, an individual was arrested and was refused medical treatment. She charged the city with failure to adequately train police officers to determine when prisoners require medical attention. The Supreme Court ruled that when the lack of training is obviously likely to lead to violations of an individual's constitutional rights, it can then be said that the lack of training is the result of deliberate indifference on the part of the city (Eyres and Moreland, 1994).

A final area of litigation is that surrounding the widespread use of employee involvement teams. Union officials charged Electromation, Inc., with using employee teams that included management representation to negotiate bargainable items. This, they said, violated the spirit of the National Labor Relations Board statutes prohibiting managers from creating management-controlled employee groups intended to bar or replace union representation. Electromation lost the suit. Turner (1995) finds that personnel directors often simply ignore this ruling since it is practically impossible to implement and flies in the face of current wisdom about the importance of using employee involvement teams.

Diffusion. The diffusion of the field affects both the professionalization of its members and the future direction of practice. Often described as marginal (Watkins, 1994), human resource development is losing clarity of function. Andersen Consulting, for example, might recruit MBAs, instructional technologists, industrial and organizational psychologists, and adult educators. The human resource department might represent only a portion of the workplace learning that is occurring. And training departments are themselves often being eliminated, spun off as profit centers or whole new businesses, or outsourced. That this is occurring during the greatest upsurge in demand for training suggests that previous organizational structures for delivering training are not working.

Training will be performed more often in the future by nontrainers, including managers, team leaders, and technical employees. Learning from one's work, self-directed learning projects, and desktop learning strategies will place responsibility for training in the hands of the learner. Responsibility for workplace learning is becoming diffused throughout many tasks, functions, and roles. This trend makes learning coterminous with work, a necessary evolution in an information era (Watkins and Marsick, 1993).

New Rules. In many organizations a new employee contract is called for that asks workers to earn their job every day. Economists ask us to prepare for a jobless economy. Security is gone, and with it any sense an employee might have of entitlement. Replacing these past verities is a new ethic of entrepreneurialism, temporary loyalty, and knowledge-driven competitive advantage. Managers find that they must get the work done in the same or less time with a workforce that feels no loyalty and is temporary, contract labor, or telecommuting. Skills leave with departing employees, and new employees must be trained constantly with no loss of production. The manager must offer something that the employee values without promising long-term employment and must persuade the employee to comply when there are few options other than to fire the noncompliant.

Employees' attitudes toward training in this context are changing. Training becomes knowledge, which is transportable—something that they can take with them wherever they go. Where employees were sent to training before, many now view this as a privilege and seek training on their own time. They take videos and audio self-help tapes home, they take courses at local colleges at night and on weekends, and they look toward their next job. These individuals are the new infopreneurs—people using information as a key to creating a new market niche for themselves.

Similarly, the workplace is increasingly one's laptop computer—wherever it is located. Says Penzias, tomorrow's interactions may depend more on shared understanding than shared office spaces, and tomorrow's leaders will create coherence through shared visions and common professional values (Penzias, 1995). Workplace learning programs will need to promote shared understanding, visions, and values.

Technology. Technology and information systems have the potential to flatten organizations and to promote widespread sharing of information. This dissemination of information in turn generates new knowledge and information and promotes organizational learning. Control shifts to the workers, who because of access to knowledge, are able to make decisions and to act. Whole communities of workers are created through information systems. People become members of virtual teams, electronic community or town hall meetings, bulletin board interest groups, chat rooms, and groupware-based brainstorming or problem-solving communities. How does one design learning for a sales force whose car is their office? Classroom training becomes an opportunity for social and personal contact. Once again, the role of workplace education is shifting to speak through these technology-driven media.

One idea that is taking hold in human resource development is that of the learning organization (Marsick and Watkins, 1994). Learning organizations require the creation of "practice fields" (Kofman and Senge, 1993) or "interstitial communities of practice" (Brown and Duguid, 1991), in which individuals socially construct knowledge or wisdom that is shared in stories. This collaboratively created knowledge creates a community of practice that evolves reciprocally; as individuals learn to become part of the community of practice, they also transform it. This quality of co-creation is a natural by-product of the changing workplace brought on by technology and is central to the idea of the learning organization.

Globalization. Surveying four hundred human resource development executives regarding trends that will affect workplace learning in the next five years, *Training and Development Journal* ("Trends That Will Influence Workplace Learning," 1994) found that the most significant trend was that of responding to the demands of the global economy. Stephen Rhinesmith (1995, p. 37) calls on us to reframe the boundaries of

- Space, time, and geography that inhibit efficiency
- Functional, professional, and technical specialties that prevent customers from getting their needs met, that are the antithesis of one-stop shopping
- Thinking and classifying that inhibit collaborative decision making and that create we-they dichotomies
- Cultural assumptions, beliefs, and values that keep us from working with others from different backgrounds.

Overcoming these boundaries is what Rhinesmith defines as *global thinking*. Training departments offer courses in global thinking, foreign languages, and managing diversity. Training materials are examined for culture friendliness. Delivery is adapted both in terms of content and mode in different cultures. Some training departments are globally dispersed, such as that at Nortel Corporation, which has members in Toronto, Raleigh, Nashville, Fort Worth, Ottawa, and London. Functions are equally differentiated, with leadership development based in Nashville but serving the global management workforce. Ford 2000 is an initiative designed to accomplish a similar end, with all Ford departments becoming merged by the year 2000. An engine built in Detroit will meet the same specifications as one built in England, and either engine will fit the Ford car of the year 2000. Employees working on automobile engines in England will be part of the same division now based in Ann Arbor, Michigan. This alignment of products will require an alignment of manufacturing, assembly, marketing, and management practices. New training approaches are needed that incorporate this global mindset.

Reengineering. While Michael Hammer has stated that reengineering has not worked, corporations continue to work to eliminate duplication and to cut personnel through a redesign of work processes. In the 1995 *Training* magazine industry survey, 35 percent of the organizations responding reported that they were engaged in reengineering ("1995 Industry Report," 1995). Not surprisingly, almost the same percentage (31 percent) said that they were currently "downsizing." When *Training and Development Journal* ("Trends That Will Influence Workplace Learning," 1994) asked executives which of thirty-six business and industry trends would have the greatest effect on human resource development, reengineering was at the top of the list. While originally a concept driven by engineers and managers, this process has been handed off to the training department. The association with a process that almost inevitably is equated with cutting staff is not likely to have a positive long-term effect on the training function.

Conclusion

These issues are changing all of education and business. What is intriguing are the ways in which these changes affect workplace education. Workplace learning strategies are helping business understand that "most competitive improvements cannot be bought; they must be learned" ("Trends That Will Influence Workplace Learning," 1994, p. S6). Gephart (1995) cites research on high-performance work systems and concludes that, taken together, the studies show that new flexible forms of work organizations, when combined with human resource management systems, can greatly enhance productivity and quality. What is needed are complementary and reinforcing work and human resource practices.

In the past, workplace learning was primarily skills training based on immediate job needs. In the future, workplace learning will become everyone's responsibility and will be integrally tied to performance and production. Where before, human resources was a parallel function, even a luxury, it will increasingly become integrated into all functions—less like school and more like work. In the increasingly complex and differentiated workplace, there will also be more emphasis on a parallel work-based credentialing system: Motorola University and Mastercard University. In these instances, it will be a replacement for school or a "post-graduate" alternative. Learning in the workplace is a major industry, with increasingly differentiated modes of delivery, providers, and functions. Skills for workplace learning facilitators will simultaneously be made more replicable by computers and nontrainers while more sophisticated skills will be expected of certain types of providers. This has been called an age of discontinuity, where trends explode in diametrically opposed directions, and the changing face of human resource development is one testament that this is an apt description for this era.

References

Brown, J., and Duguid, P. "Organizational Learning and Communities of Practice: Toward a Unified View of Working, Learning, and Innovation." *Organization Science,* 1991, 2 (1), 40–57.

Carnevale, A., and Carnevale, E. "Growth Patterns in Workplace Training." *Training and Development Journal,* 1994, 48 (5), S22–S28.

Carnevale, A., Gainer, L., and Villet, J. *Training in America: The Organization and Strategic Role of Training.* San Francisco: Jossey-Bass, 1990.

"The Coming of Age of Workplace Learning: A Time Line." *Training and Development Journal,* 1994, 48 (5), S5–S12.

Eyres, P., and Moreland, W. *Training and Legal Issues.* Amherst, Mass.: HRD Press, 1994.

Gephart, M. "The Road to High Performance." *Training and Development Journal,* 1995, *49* (6), 29–44.

Goldstein, I. *Training in Organizations: Needs Assessment, Development and Evaluation.* (2nd ed.) Pacific Grove, Calif.: Brooks/Cole, 1986.

Hicks, I. "Forgotten Voice: Women in Organizational Development and Human Resource Development." Unpublished dissertation, University of Texas, Austin, 1991.

Kofman, F., and Senge, P. "Communities of Commitment: The Heart of Learning Organizations." *Organizational Dynamics,* 1993, *3,* 5–23.

McLagan, P. *Models for Excellence.* Alexandria, Va.: ASTD Press, 1993.

Marsick, V. J., and Watkins, K. "The Learning Organization: An Integrative Vision for HRD." *Human Resource Development Quarterly,* 1994, *5* (4), 353–360.

Nadler, L., and Nadler, Z. *Developing Human Resources: Concepts and a Model.* (3rd ed.) San Francisco: Jossey-Bass, 1989.

"1995 Industry Report." *Training,* 1995, *32* (10), 37–82.

Penzias, A. *Harmony.* New York: HarperCollins, 1995.

Resnick, L. "Learning in School and Out." *Educational Researcher,* 1987, *16* (9), 13–20.

Rhinesmith, S. "Open the Door to a Global Mindset." *Training and Development Journal,* 1995, *49* (5), 35–43.

Rothwell, W., and Kazanas, H. *Human Resource Development: A Strategic Approach.* Amherst, Mass.: HRD Press, 1994.

Swanson, R., and Torraco, R. "The History of Technical Training." In L. Kelly (ed.), *The ASTD Technical and Skills Training Handbook.* New York: McGraw-Hill, 1995.

"Trends That Will Influence Workplace Learning and Performance in the Next Five Years." *Training and Development Journal,* 1994, *48* (5), S29–S31.

Turner, B. *Legal Issues in Human Resource Development.* Austin: University of Texas, 1995.

Watkins, K. *Facilitating Learning in the Workplace.* Geelong, Canada: Deakin University Press, 1991.

Watkins, K. "On Being Both Academic and Relevant." *Human Resource Development Quarterly,* 1994, *5* (4), 297–300.

Watkins, K., and Marsick, V. J. *Sculpting the Learning Organization: Lessons in the Art and Science of Systematic Change.* San Francisco: Jossey-Bass, 1993.

Watkins, K., and Marsick, V. J. *In Action: The Learning Organization.* Alexandria, Va.: American Society for Training and Development, in press.

Yost, E. *Frank and Lillian Gilbreth: Partners for Life.* New Brunswick, N.J.: Rutgers University Press, 1949.

KAREN E. WATKINS is associate professor of adult education at the University of Georgia and president of the Academy of Human Resource Development.

This chapter provides a work-in-progress definition of the workforce development system and frames issues and questions for national and state policy makers on how to develop such a system.

Workforce Development: The Policy Debate

Joan L. Wills

The term *workforce development system* is new in the rhetoric of the policy discussions. The attention given to the establishment of a workforce development system has clearly been incremental. The various components have evolved slowly. There have been decades when little happened followed by periods of almost frenzied activity and expansion. We are currently in one of those periods of discussion and action. It remains to be seen whether we will eventually develop a national consensus and infrastructure of programs to promote the skill development of members of the workforce.

It is doubtful that there is even agreement on what the term *workforce development system* means. For the purpose of this chapter, it means the overarching framework that includes the structure, legislative authority, and core implementation strategies used by all the stakeholders in the systems. The structure needs governance bodies that set goals, outcomes, indicators of progress, benchmarks of best practice, and processes for delivery of services. The framework includes the *formal* links between the separate public and private (if using government funds) governance structures (such as kindergarten through grade 12, postsecondary schooling, training bodies, state agencies, and local units of government). The workforce development system includes a subsystem focused on initial preparation of the labor force, that is, the school-to-work or school-to-career subsystem. This subsystem must also be linked to a broader network that incorporates other purposes of education, such as preparing for the responsibilities of citizenship. There are other

Barbara Kaufman, a senior associate of the Center for Workforce Development, provided useful comments on this chapter.

subsystems that include the continual preparation of the current workforce. Another subsystem comprises employment-related services such as labor market information, job matching, and placement.

The workforce development system must utilize tools, such as information and accountability procedures that have the capacity to cross-reference data between the subsystems. Staff responsible for a specific component within any part of a subsystem need to understand how the pieces of the overall system support their own work. Additionally, the staff of the various parts need to be rewarded for assisting in the achievement of the overall goals and specific benchmarks of progress relevant to their own work. In other words, the professional development of the staffs is a core implementation concern whatever the structure and legislative authority framework may be.

On the basis of this definition, it must be said we do not have such a system in the United States today. However, we do have a base to build on. Congress is considering the establishment of such a system. The shape and form are being vigorously debated. One of the key questions is what will be the national infrastructure that ties the work of the states and localities and hundreds of thousands of institutions together. Congress is working from a base of programs it has supported to construct such a system. It is facing a daunting task. As programs sponsored by the federal government have evolved over the years, there is a set of themes that have permeated each round of debate and implementation of the resulting programs. Each has influenced the current structure, legislative framework, and implementation practices. Questions and issues requiring resolution are multiple. Many have been on the table for decades and have remained unsettled.

What should be the appropriate governance structure? Who should establish the overarching structure of a workforce development system? Congress? A national body composed of representative stakeholders of the system? If there is to be a national stakeholder group, who should appoint it, and what should its range of responsibilities include? What should be the role of the federal government versus that of the states? Should there be a direct line between federally selected service providers and federal government, or can the services be delivered by a range of organizations? Within the states, the questions center on the relationships between the general units of government relationship and the separate educational governance structure and the relationships between the state and substate units of general or education authorities. Is there a need for a local-level decision-making body? If so, what should its responsibilities and its relationship to locally elected officials be? Should it have the ultimate decision-making authority over the selection of service providers? To whom should it be accountable? What special role should be accorded to specific stakeholders, such as the employer community, in the governance structure? What role should be given to representatives of client groups, such as the disabled and minority communities?

How should the funds be targeted? Should a workforce development system be designed as a universal one, available to all individuals? Who should pay for the universal services: individuals, employers, the public? If the public should pay, which level of government should administer the funding? Should some services be universal and others not? These questions have no obvious answers, but need to be explicitly debated and resolved as a workforce development system unfolds.

Over time, choices have been made at the federal level regarding targeting. With the exception of job search support and initial vocational education, almost no federal program has enjoyed universal coverage. Various means have been utilized to target the resources, such as specific geographic areas, employment status (mainly unemployed), education deficit, physical or mental disability, and at-risk status, such as incarceration or teen pregnancy. By far, the most common targeting tool of workforce development programs has been the income status of the individual. It is unlikely that any time soon the pattern of targeting federal programs will be changed significantly (though the states may have some authority to move some targeted money among subpopulation groups).

How should quality of program service be measured, and by whom? For programs funded by the federal government there has always been a monitoring role. However for programs that include state or local funds there has always been a lack of clarity regarding ultimate responsibility for establishing the quality indicators. Additionally, the measurement tools to determine quality have until very recently predominately focused on input measures, not output. For example, input measures such as teacher-pupil ratios and library facilities have been used to judge quality as opposed to the knowledge and skills gained by students. Should market forces be used as the primary tool to establish quality? Use of market forces implies, in part, that consumers, or at least adult consumers, should be allowed to make their own choices of services through the use of vouchers.

How should accountability for the use of the funds be ensured? Fiscal management and fiduciary responsibilities were for a long time the primary focus of accountability systems. Over the years, this emphasis proved to be insufficient and the idea of performance standards emerged as a companion device to track the work of a service provider. However, performance standards have often had to rely on measures of success that can be strongly influenced by uncontrollable factors such as job placement rates in the middle of a recession. Additionally, outcome-based information has simply not existed either within states or nationally.

As different forms of targeting for determining eligibility have grown, it has become a substantial administrative and accountability burden at the operational level for all of the programs, and it has had the unintended consequence across the country of reducing the popularity of the programs with those who are responsible for administering them.

Throughout all the accountability efforts, there remain questions about who the accountability is to. The federal government? State government? The local school board? Others? Who should have the lead in establishing the indicators of success and progress? Who should reward success?

What should be the range of services provided? The types of services that can be paid for through federal funds have often varied widely over the course of any grant-in-aid program. There have been two countervailing forces at work. Individuals responsible for general policy often want as few required services as possible written into the law, while advocates for a particular service or a particular population push for specifics in the type and form of the service to be provided. When originally passed, legislation contains less specific language, but the allowable activities become tighter in subsequent reauthorization. Quite often tighter reins are established in response to lessons learned about what works or to correct a problem perceived to be damaging to the program's credibility.

Another form of targeting that has been used for administrative purposes is the preselection of specific institutions to deliver a specified set of services for a particular cohort of individuals, for example, public schools, vocational rehabilitation, and labor exchange agencies. This preferred provider mechanism has been a source of many debates at all levels of government and among various stakeholder groups. In response to these debates, an array of mandated coordination requirements were inserted into federal legislation. Mandated coordination has normally meant review and sign-off on each other's plans as they are submitted to the federal government.

Who should be responsible for collecting and managing program service information? One of the most critical implementation issues is how to collect, share, and use information about the people being served and the organizations providing the services. Who should be responsible for deciding what information is needed and for what purposes it is used is a governance issue. Information clearly affects any legislative debate and needs to be used by service providers for administrative tracking and monitoring purposes. Consensus exists that the federal government should have the lead responsibility for the collection of general social and economic data, but there has been a continual and growing tension about the proper role of the federal government in the collection of program and administrative information.

Every program has had a specific management information system attached to it over the years, but the quality of data has often been called into question as well as the appropriateness of the tasks needed to collect and monitor information. A major problem has been that the staff who are responsible for direct interactions with the client have not felt any value in the information collected because the systems have not been designed to help them do their job better.

In addition, little attention has been given to the need of consumers of information—students, parents, employers, and other consumers—when information systems have been designed. A particular problem is that information about types of services and programs available from *all* government workforce development programs is not available in any user-friendly fashion.

Who should be responsible for ensuring the staff providing the services are adequately prepared? Another key implementation issue is helping the staffs of a wide range of institutions understand not just their specific jobs but also how the pieces fit together in a workforce preparation system. This is no small task. State and local civil service exams and the certification and licensure systems of education and rehabilitation systems are used to determine who is at least minimally qualified for initial hiring. However, these screens have been proven to be insufficient for the continual professional development demands of the service providers staff. The federal government has long provided technical assistance for the staffs of individual programs, but there has been a growing body of evidence that a more focused effort of continual professional development is necessary. Who should be responsible for this is an unsettled issue. The individuals? The organizations for which they work? The state? The federal government?

In 1995 all of these issues were on the table, along with an overarching question about which level of government should be responsible for financing what types of programs. This chapter will not focus on the fiscal federalism portion of the mighty debates that are occurring. Reducing the federal deficit, which grew to staggering proportions in the 1980s, is clearly important, but the amount of dollars alone does not tell the story. Indeed, it appears that fiscal federalism issues are often used to obfuscate—rather than clarify—the appropriate roles of different stakeholders in the organization of a workforce development system.

While it is true we have long had a general consensus that workforce preparation requires a national infrastructure, there has been little agreement about the overall goals. How should it be organized? Who should be responsible for deciding what its functions are and how its success is to be measured? Until very recently the answers to the questions have been to create separate programs, or "silos," with independent constituencies. The term *nonsystem* is often used to describe the current state of affairs. The lack of clarity is clearly feeding the debates in Congress.

A Brief Walk Through History

To understand the current debate about the establishment of a workforce development system requires a look back. The federal government has seldom mounted a new education or training program that has not already been at least partially developed within several states. It is equally true that reports and study groups have helped form federal actions.

In the last half of the nineteenth century, the states established manual labor schools that combined occupational preparation with the "mental" training that had been the domain of public schools. By the end of the first decade of the twentieth century, most states had provided for some form of industrial education. The apprenticeship model that combined intellectual and manual arts was adapted to become a school-based work preparation program. The federal government first became involved through direct appropriations for education through the Smith-Hughes Act in 1917, whose success was spurred on by World War I. Public education advocates and agricultural and industrial interests finally came together to convince Congress of the need for legislation to promote vocational preparation in industrial arts, and agricultural and domestic sciences (home economics for females). The bulk of the funds were used for the direct payment of salaries of specialized teachers.

Just three years later the physically disabled population was recognized as needing targeted services and the Vocational Rehabilitation (VR) system was created. The VR system has used the state government as its administrative arm, and the federal government has been deeply involved in oversight of the organization, including establishing the job duties of the direct service staff.

Expansion Phase 1: The 1930s to the 1950s. It was not until the Great Depression that more federal support for members of the workforce was forthcoming. The emphasis in the 1930s did not predominantly focus on training; instead, the thrust was income support and job creation. The activist Roosevelt administration used a three-pronged strategy to support the workforce during this distressful period. The job-creation strategies included a wide range of new initiatives, such as the Civilian Conservation Corps and the Works Progress Administration. These programs were intended to be temporary and disappeared during the war years. Two types of income support strategies employed at that time have become more permanent features of our intergovernmental support system. The first was for widows, orphans, and the disabled, the precursor to the now maligned Aid for Families with Dependent Children (AFDC) entitlement program. The second was a wage replacement program, the Unemployment Insurance program, which was financed by payroll taxes. There were substantial debates at the time of passage of all of these pieces of legislation about the proper balance between the role of the federal government versus that of the states.

In 1937 training requirements of craft workers were given a boost by the enactment of the National Apprenticeship Act. A model of brevity, the law contains just five paragraphs. Employers pay for the training and many consider it a private-sector program, not public program. The related instruction requirement for apprenticeship is delivered by both secondary and postsecondary school, as well as by employers and correspondence schools. The government's role includes development, in cooperation with industry, of apprenticeship standards that meet federal and state (where appropriate) guidelines. However, the definitions of standards and the measures used to define quality are not firm and relate to Equal Employment Opportunities requirements, wage rates to be paid to apprentices, and ratios of apprentices to journey workers at the worksite. The apprentice training model remains the smallest form of training in the United States. According to the U.S. Department of Labor's Bureau of Apprenticeship, only about 1.6 million people have completed apprenticeships since 1950.

After World War II, a variety of services were made available for veterans. The GI bill, a voucher program, allowed individuals to choose which postsecondary education institution they would attend. The Veterans Administration, the federal agency responsible for the oversight of the legislation, established some quality control systems for the program. Postsecondary institutions were "certified" by the Veterans Administration in order to be eligible to accept students.

Vestiges of that certification—or quality assurance system—remain today in the management of the student grant and loan programs administered by the U.S. Department of Education. Today's version of quality assurance for postsecondary institutions includes the requirement that the institution show proof that it has been accredited by a regional or national voluntary accreditation body prior to accepting students. These "self-regulatory" bodies are a part of a national network that was voluntarily established by representatives of the institutions themselves. Most states have chosen to use these various accreditation organizations as a part of their own quality assurance processes.

"Veterans' preferences" went beyond the right to a GI voucher after the war. A form of targeting was introduced. An array of special services were developed, including hiring bonuses for those who had served their country. These preferences continue yet today, and many are administered by the Employment Services within the states.

Expansion Phase 2: The 1960s. The 1960s generated a major expansion of workforce development initiatives. Two separate strands of public concern propelled the federal government into action. The first was concern with the role of technological change and the high levels of unemployment that persisted after the Korean war. The second was the concern about the number of people of minorities, mostly African Americans, who were not able to obtain the jobs that would raise them out of poverty.

The Soviet Union's launching of Sputnik was a blow to the pride of the United States. This helped spur a willingness for the federal government to take action to address the technical capabilities of the workforce. The Manpower Development and Training Act (MDTA) was passed in 1962. MDTA used the chain of authority that had been established in the 1930s: the state labor exchange agencies (the Employment Services) were charged with the responsibility to work with the state agency responsible for the vocational education programs to jointly administer the program. In most states this early effort of mandated coordination between separate agencies did not work well. The essence of the mandated coordination was the Employment Service, which was responsible for determining the training needs, and the vocational education agency was to ensure that the training occurred in one of the educational institutions recognized by the state. Using only one source of information to determine the demand for skill training has never proven to be popular among educators and is not always accurate.

The 1960s found another set of forces in country. The economic boom time of the postwar period for most Americans generated a willingness to address the ongoing problems facing many citizens. The effects of racial discrimination and poverty on the underclass were finally considered to be intolerable sores on the fabric of society. The Great Society programs began to pour forth. A major portion of these programs placed substantial emphasis on education and training of the workforce. Most of these programs bypassed state and local governments and went directly to newly created community-based organizations and local school districts for their management. At that time state governments were considered a part of the problem and not a part of the solution to correct the root causes of discrimination and poverty. The programs that emerged through this war on poverty helped to generate a mix of service providers and oversight advisory groups that continue today in many communities throughout the country.

The period of the last half of the 1960s and the early 1970s was one of great activity in Washington. Legislative oversight and changes in the federal grant-in-aid programs became more frequent, and several new programs were established each year. Concerns about proliferation, accountability, and quality came to the forefront. Governors and big-city mayors were leading a parade calling for more control and coherence. However, there was little agreement between the elected officials within the states about where the authority should rest—at the state or local level.

When President Nixon came into office, in part to fulfill his campaign pledge for "new federalism," discussions moved to consolidation of programs and new mechanisms to promote accountability. Local elected officials were the big winners at that time in the workforce development arena, with the states given the responsibility to manage programs in the sparsely populated rural areas and some coordination tasks. The Comprehensive Employment and Training Act (CETA) combined several of the war on poverty programs with the MDTA but did not include the labor exchange services managed by the state Employment Service, the successors to the 1917 vocational education legislation, vocational rehabilitation, the adult education program, or the employment-related service programs for welfare recipients. In other words, the term *comprehensive* in the act was more of a hyperbole than a fact. No consensus emerged regarding the appropriate roles of the three levels of government. Nor was any consensus developed about the particular responsibilities of the separate education governance system for the K–12 and postsecondary education institutions, nor who would be responsible for reconciling the differences between the various state agencies or the demands of various stakeholders (such as businesses and unions). Without such agreements the development of a coherent sequence of services for the clients was never able to be realized, nor was it possible to construct an accountability system that withstood a hard look.

During this same period there were other efforts to establish a national presence in the schools to help young people make more informed choices about their future life in the workforce. A form of targeting and promotion of certain types of activities was embedded in the Career Education Act. This act was in part an attempt to provide new forms of instruction in the schools that would give a young person experiential learning opportunities, including some time spent in the workplace. (This legislation did not survive the Reagan consolidation drive in the next decade, though one can still find remnants of the programs it promulgated in some schools.)

The States Reemerge: The 1980s and 1990s. The 1980s witnessed a major resurgence of state government activism. Governors and state legislators increasingly turned their attention to the issue of education and training. In large measure, this attention was driven by employers, mostly in the southern states and in large urban northern communities that cited the lack of preparedness of young people for the world of work. They, the governors and state legislative leaders, thought that the economic competitiveness of the states was being threatened because of the apparent poor quality of the K–12 education system. The causes and effects continue to be debated, but there is no doubt the elected political leaders did respond to the call to improve their economic competitiveness. An explosion of new programs were enacted in almost all of the states not only to upgrade the K–12 education system but also to increase the retraining of current workers.

The federal response to the issues surrounding workforce development systems during the 1980s was in large measure driven by the belief system of President Reagan. Devolution was the talk of Washington during much of his time in office. Little agreement was reached about what devolution really meant. A great many proposals emanated from the executive branch of the federal government to eliminate a large number of programs and reduce federal expenditures simultaneously. Another round of grant consolidations did occur under the Reagan period. This was due, in part, to the then conspicuous pattern of Congress adding small categorical programs to the intergovernmental grant-in-aid system—most often promulgated by state or local officials. CETA was replaced with the Job Training Partnership Act (JTPA). The job creation portion of CETA, the largest component, was totally eliminated, leaving support for training and related services. JTPA continued the pattern, begun in the war on poverty programs, of using economic status as the primary eligibility criterion for individuals to participate. There was some recognition, however, that income could not be the only determinate of training needs, so a new dislocated workers program was included in the JTPA legislation, by which an individual's employment status (unemployed for a certain length of time) triggered eligibility.

Through the passage of JTPA, state government was given a stronger role, as was the business community. The Reagan administration built on a demonstration project begun by President Carter that gave a "controlling voice" over the mandated Private Industry Councils that had to be established in local areas. The federal legislation gave Private Industry Councils a broad range of responsibilities to coordinate all the job preparation programs within their geographic area.

States absorbed much of the grant management functions that had been the federal government's responsibilities for the substate service delivery areas. For the first time in a piece of federal legislation, performance standards became a part of the accountability system. The federal government was charged with establishing the core standards, and governors were allowed to make "in state" modifications, if approved by the U.S. Secretary of Labor.

Another major feature of the JTPA legislation was that it amended, for the first time since its original enactment, the Wagner-Peyser Act. Governors were given oversight authority over the program of services. Prior to this change, the U.S. Employment Service essentially treated states as their administrative agents. The undergirding philosophy of the labor exchange services (job matching, placement, and labor market information) is a need for common services across state lines. The JTPA amendments to the Wagner-Peyser Act did not erase the recognition for a national infrastructure of common services, but did give more management flexibility to the states. Like CETA, JTPA did not address governance or accountability relationships with other federally funded programs focused on workforce development. Exhortations to coordinate and sign off on each other's plans were a nod to interdependency. These exhortations only focused on labor exchange, work/welfare programs, and vocational education, but not vocational rehabilitation, apprenticeship, or services to veterans.

During the Bush administration a significant welfare-related education and training program was enacted. The work/welfare legislation built on a very small (around $200 million) stand-alone work preparation program for welfare recipients called WIN that had been a part of the original war on poverty legislation in the 1960s. A major push by the nation's governors (with then Governor Bill Clinton in a lead role) resulted in the passage of the JOBS program. Hailed as a major breakthrough that would change welfare dependency forever, the JOBS program substantially increased the amount of available dollars; the hope was that the federal government's support would reach $1.3 billion in 1995, with states supplementing this amount with up to approximately 40 percent more. (Most states did not allocate the necessary matching dollars, and the full federal authorization has not been tapped).

For the first time, federal law mandated that education services be made available to welfare recipients in welfare-to-work programs. It also specified states must guarantee child care for every AFDC parent who is satisfactorily participating in an approved education, training, and employment activity.

The federal JOBS legislation is built on the concept that a social contract must be written between the client and the government outlining mutual responsibilities. This paradigm shift replaces a top-down dictate from the federal government about which agency should be responsible for which set of services. JOBS gives local officials more freedom to organize services as they see fit, yet at the same time it is establishing new forms of accountability to ensure that institutions deliver to the clients appropriate and cost-effective services. JOBS shifts the criterion from inputs to be coordinated to outputs to be judged.

Another grant consolidation effort occurred in 1991 when Congress passed the Omnibus Literacy Act to improve the knowledge base of what are the most effective approaches to providing basic education and workforce literacy for adults. A new work-based literacy program national competitive grant program was authorized in response to employers' concerns regarding poor literacy skills. However, the bulk of the increased funds continue to flow through the states and the twenty-plus-year-old Adult Basic Education program. Performance standards were to be established for the first time and developed in conjunction with the other workforce preparation programs (JTPA, JOBS, Vocational Education). Linkages are expected between JTPA and JOBS programs, and the states are required to use a competitive bid process. Prior to this time, the funds flowed somewhat automatically to preselected education institutions (either local education agencies or community colleges). The new competition rules require that community-based organizations have "direct and equitable access" to the state basic grant.

Commissions and Study Groups. Perhaps because the nation has lacked a workforce development structure, there has been a heavy reliance on commissions and study groups to make recommendations about how to draw the stands together. Congressionally mandated studies or executive branch ad hoc blue ribbon commissions are commonplace. Foundations have supported an array of such study groups as well.

An example is the Commission on Technology and the American Economy, established in the mid-1960s. Its findings and recommendations still have currency. The report issued by the Commission during the time Willard Wirtz was Secretary of Labor has had long-term influence on our labor market programs. Not all of its recommendations were adopted, such as establishing a national guaranteed income floor for those who could not care for themselves and expanding the concept of the agriculture extension service to universities and other organizations for the purpose of helping businesses and governments stimulate technological innovations and make the adjustments when dislocation occurred.

The commission felt that our country had an education system far superior to those of other countries and the concern therefore needed to be ensuring that everyone had access to the system. It believed that the role of government was most appropriately targeted to assisting those who did not have adequate education opportunities (they recommended that everyone be given access to free education for fourteen years) and assisting selected geographic areas where there were high levels of poverty or dislocation.

The commission had major concerns about how the delivery systems should be designed. It questioned the capacity of municipalities to organize and manage services in labor market areas and therefore urged the federal government to establish an overlay of area-wide planning and delivery networks across the country. It recommended that the Employment Service be both federalized and given the lead responsibility in managing this national network. (The Employment Service was not federalized, but it was given the lead responsibilities at that time in managing the Department of Labor programs.) What is striking when one reads this dated report is how little the issues have changed—with the exception of the belief that we have the best education system in the world.

The 1980s may go down in history as the decade of reports. There were a substantial number of reports searching for better answers. Multiple research reports and commission documents prepared at the state and federal level or generated by ad hoc groups of luminaries all contributed to a clarion call for improving education. For example, *A Nation at Risk: The Imperative for Education Reform* (National Commission on Excellence in Education, 1983), issued by the U.S. Department of Education in 1983, set a broad agenda for upgrading academic levels. The report galvanized education reform efforts all over the country, and state and local reports mimicking it were produced all over the country. Shortly after the release of that report, the ad hoc National Commission on Secondary Vocational Education was called together by vocational education leaders, and its report, *The Unfinished Agenda: The Role of Vocational Education in High School,* was issued by the National Center for Research in Vocational Education in 1984. A key reason for its issuance was a strong feeling on the part of the vocational education community that *A Nation at Risk* was elitist in its thrust 'and undervalued the important role high schools play in preparing young people for work.

One of the actions resulting from *A Nation at Risk* was a collective effort of the nation's governors. Through the National Governors' Association (1986) *Time for Results* was issued, which outlined a set of specific actions each state should employ to improve the education system. A tracking system was instituted by the association to monitor the follow-up activities in each state. This work led to an education summit between the governors and President Bush. The eventual outcome of that summit was the establishment of the National Education Goals Panel, which established six overarching goals for education (a seventh was added in 1994). Workforce preparation issues are embedded in the ambitious Goal 6, which sets out that "by the year 2000, every adult American will be literate and will possess the knowledge and skills necessary to compete in a global economy and exercise the rights and responsibilities of citizenship." Included in the objectives to be met is a call for every major business to be involved in strengthening the connection between education and work. Short of a miracle, the goal will not be met by the turn of the century. Yet, since their adoption the establishment of all the goals has served as the focal point for the work of the federal government and many of the states.

Other influential reports, such as *The Neglected Majority,* by Dale Parnell (1985), and *The Forgotten Half: Non-College Youth in America,* by the William T. Grant Foundation Commission on Work, Family, and Citizenship (1988), noted the importance of paying attention to the workforce preparation responsibilities of the education enterprise. At about the same time, the Department of Labor weighed in with *Workforce 2000: Work and Workers for the 21st Century* (Johnston and Packer, 1987) and *Workplace Basics: The Essential Skills Employers Want* (Carnevale, Gainer, and Meltzer, 1990), a study from the American Society of Training and Development supported by the Department of Labor. These sent out the message that the requirements of the workplace had changed and that the content of education and training programs therefore had to adjust.

A common key message from these reports was that the nation needed to substantially rethink how we allocate vocational preparation resources, prepare curricula and deliver instruction, and provide individuals with the tools for the workplace of tomorrow. For the first time in our history, the conversations and debate began to center on efforts for systemic change.

The search for a more coherent workforce development framework led many American policy makers to other countries to benchmark our practices against those of our economic competitors. These exercises yielded the understanding that while each country has its own unique set of processes and programs to prepare the workforce, other countries have common features that have been essentially missing in this country. Our economic competitors have national systems (which include roles for subnational units of government in recognition of regional variations) that engage all of the stakeholders—industry, unions, education and training institutions, and so on—in the process of determining the skill requirements of the workplace, awarding credentials to individuals, and articulating the occupation-focused curriculums. In many of these countries, there are formal processes and agreements with industry to share the governance and management of the schooling process for occupation-specific training. In other words, they have focused their attention on core functions of a workforce preparation system: assisting individuals to gain the knowledge and skills necessary for them to be productive members of the workforce.

The members of the Commission on the Skills of the American Workforce, which issued the 1990 report *America's Choice: High Skills or Low Wages!* believed that the United States should establish formal processes, systems, and structures that would involve industries in the development and implementation of education and training for large portions of the workforce.

In response to these calls for change, the Bush administration established the Secretary's Commission on the Necessary Skills (SCANS) and the National Advisory Commission on Work-Based Learning (NACWBL). The SCANS commissioners provided a powerful taxonomy to describe the basic and foundation skills needed to participate in the workplace of the future.

NACWBL laid the groundwork, supporting the development of a national voluntary system to promote the use of skill standards. This included using the authority under the Perkins II legislation to promote industry-driven skill standards. National trade associations such as Automotive Service Excellence and the Associated General Contractors had advocated that the federal government support standards development. These organizations have been working voluntarily for a number of years with state vocational education leaders to improve the occupational education and training efforts of schools.

Current Building Blocks

In 1994 three pieces of federal legislation were approved that are intertwined in purpose and actions: the School-to-Work Opportunities Act (STWO) of 1994; the promotion of national education reform through the Goals 2000:

Educate America Act; and within the Goals 2000 legislation, Title V, which established the National Skills Standards Act. Each represent capacity-building and infrastructure development opportunities. Each reflects an effort to build and strengthen the base of current institutions while creating new links between those institutions.

The three pieces of legislation do not mandate any specific requirements to be placed on any state or locality. They promote change through voluntary actions. The linchpin of the systemic change strategy of the three pieces is the development of standards.

Why Standards? The decentralized governance system and reliance on a multitude of public and private institutions to assist in the education and training in the United States generate substantial communication challenges. The development of standards is to help address this "boundary impediment." The hope is that using standards as a tool can link the respective strengths of all the institutions engaged in the workforce preparation enterprise. Standards help ensure quality, indicate goals, and promote change. Standards can facilitate communications and center the work on one of the most crucial outputs of workforce preparation programs, regardless of the source of funding.

Skill Standards. The development of integrating skill standards into the instruction and assessment of students and workers is an emerging workforce development subsystem that will specifically focus on documenting the knowledge and skills required over an individual's life time in chosen occupations and providing a set of industry-valued assessments and certifications.

A major element of the National Skill Standards Act is the creation of the National Skill Standards Board (NSSB). The NSSB's mission is ambitious. Its members are to construct a voluntary system of skill standards in such a fashion that nearly all institutions concerned with worker skills would eventually be effected. Key tasks of the NSSB include identification of broad occupational clusters for skill standards around which to organize the voluntary system and recognition of partnership bodies that will have the responsibility for validating skill requirements and promoting credentials. Standards are to provide credentials (through formal assessments), and they are to be used by institutions of higher education, employers, trade associations, unions, and school-to-work programs.

The Bush administration did the preliminary work for a national system to promote the voluntary use of skill standards. The departments of Labor and Education funded twenty-two pilot projects that could potentially cover approximately 19 percent of our total occupations. These knowledge-development projects are still under way, and some will continue in the years ahead.

Academic Standards. Goals 2000 establishes voluntary national education goals to promote coherent systemic education reform and to clearly define federal, state, and local responsibilities. The work has already begun regarding what students should know on leaving grades 4, 8, and 12. The Bush administration launched the effort to develop academic standards in a range of disciplines, including science, mathematics, English, geography, arts, history, and civics, by funding professional organizations representing these disciplines. While there has been criticism of this effort, there must be some value in the work because forty-seven out of the fifty states are using the standards as a benchmark for their own work. The Goals 2000 legislation defined three types of standards: *content standards* refer to the "broad descriptions of the knowledge and skill students should acquire in a particular subject"; *performance standards* are "concrete examples and explicit definitions of what students have to know and be able to do to demonstrate that such students are proficient in the terms and knowledge framed by content standards"; and *opportunity-to-learn standards* are "the criteria for, and the basis of assessing the sufficiency or quality of the resources, practices, and conditions necessary at each level of education systems (schools, local education agencies, and States) to provide all students with an opportunity to learn the material in voluntary national content standards" (*Goals 2000: Educate America Act,* 1994, Sec. 3, Definitions).

Standards of the third type, opportunity-to-learn, have been the most controversial from the very beginning of the legislative debate. They were not supported by the Clinton administration or the political and educational leaders in the states; they were, however, supported by the Democratic leadership in Congress and many education reform advocates. With the arrival of the new Republican leadership in Congress, this language began to be stripped from the books. In keeping with our tradition, we consider them too intrusive into local control of the schools.

School-to-Work. To encourage systemic reforms, the School-to-Work Opportunities Act set out to reverse the current fragmented approach within the initial preparation subsystem. The act is jointly administered by the departments of Education and Labor (a first for the United States). Strategies to offer school-based learning connected directly to work-based learning are envisioned for all students, not just those in vocational education. The intention is to shorten the preparation time it takes students to become proficient and career-directed workers, to blend and focus the academic and contextual learning processes for career preparation for all students regardless of the setting where knowledge and skills are attained, to establish value-added credentials for both the worker and the employers to use, to create more efficient mechanisms for employers to communicate knowledge requirements to both workers and educators, and to enhance the economic competitiveness of communities as well as public and private enterprises.

Two school-to-work tools, the program of study and portable credentials, legislatively represent important changes in our intergovernmental system. For the first time in our history, there is national recognition that it is necessary to focus on knowledge and skills needed in the workplace as the key way to organize the activities at the local level.

The programs of study build on the concept of the Technical Preparation program that was promoted by the vocational education legislation amendments of 1990. The programs of study are broader in scope, but they are still to link the academic and vocational contents together. The programs of study are to be organized around career majors for occupations and through a coherent sequence of courses that ignore boundaries between institutions (such as between high school and community college or community-based organizations). The programs are to delineate what is to be learned in the workplace and how that learning relates to what occurs in the classroom, and they are to incorporate the knowledge and skill requirements of industry that have been validated nationally.

The skill certificate is defined as "a portable, industry-recognized credential" that certifies that a student has mastered levels that are at least as challenging as skill standards endorsed by the NSSB. Until the NSSB has national standards in place, the states will use their own process for issuing a credential.

The Near Future

The Clinton administration came into office with a commitment to promote an increase in both education and training initiatives. The legislation discussed in the previous section represented a first round. Increased appropriations were requested in education and training, and legislative actions were proposed. The 104th Congress has responded by proposing some of the most dramatic alterations in workforce preparation programs in this century. Sorting through the different approaches and agendas is not easy.

Currently three groups are seeking dominance in the legislative debates around a workforce development system in the nation's capital. It is unclear what the outcome will be regarding a workforce development system for the United States. The first group is operating from a belief centered on the assertion that nothing federally supported works. They see little value or need for the federal government even to be involved in almost any form. This belief is advanced by many of the recently elected members of Congress and other Republicans who have been in office longer but until 1995 were relatively powerless as members of the minority party. They are the "withdraw contingent," which in 1996 controlled the appropriations and budget committees and most of the leadership positions in the House of Representatives.

Another set of beliefs can be found among some governors and other state officials who believe that the federal monies are needed but that it is time for the federal government to withdraw from setting the direction and monitoring the work of the states. This group does not want references in the legislation to any special role for substate governments or other organizations, and they do not want any but the most minimal references to the activities to be allowed by the enabling legislation. They are the "large block grant contingent" and believe the state should be the unit of government responsible for establishing the workforce development system, including the accountability processes. This group of governors have sympathetic federal legislative friends in both the House and the Senate. The large block grant contingent has little interest in recognizing the particular needs of the physically disabled or the illiterate or in distinguishing between the needs of youth and those of adults. Nor are they interested in making distinctions by function, such as initial classroom training versus labor exchange services. In the purest form, the large block grant contingent would have Congress consolidate all of the 160-plus large and small workforce-related programs into one block grant and turn the responsibility over to the states, with them only promising to report back to the federal government on how they organized the effort and how they disbursed the money.

The third group, represented by many legislators, the federal executive branch, several key business organizations, other governors, representatives of local government, and a great number of national associations, is the "allowable activities contingent." This group makes for strange bedfellows in that they have not often worked together but are learning that they do share common interest. The allowable activities contingent is not opposed to grant consolidation per se—in fact, many in it are highly supportive of system improvement—but it is concerned about the purpose and use clauses in any legislation. For example, in this contingent one would not find many proponents wanting to mix workforce education and training services for welfare recipients with vocational education services in a high school or community college. Yet most members of this group recognize a need for recasting the workforce preparation services supported by the federal government because there is common recognition that the current forms of resource allocation, accountability, targeting, and governance mechanisms lack coherence. Their thrust is to reorganize and build on the lessons learned from the past. Of course, which lessons from the past should receive the most weight is the subject of much debate as legislation is developed. Some are inclined to focus on governance structures, while others are more concerned about the types of services that are to be provided with the funds (for example, support services such as day care, classroom instruction, and career counseling).

Many in this group have a set of concerns about building a national infrastructure based on mutually agreed on goals and knowledge standards for a workforce development system. The 1994-enacted Goals 2000: Educate America Act and School-to-Work Opportunities Act (discussed above), which focus on system development and improvement, are reflective of the type of legislation that many in the allowable activities contingent value.

The authorizing committees of both the House and the Senate are led by Republicans who fall somewhere in between the large block grant and allowable activities contingents. Each has chosen to propose the largest consolidation of workforce development programs in this century. Both have blurred the distinctions between education and training. Furthermore, the governance systems that have promoted the direct line of authority from the federal agency to the direct provider are not being protected any longer.

Activities now under way in Congress will greatly affect the near-term structure of the workforce development system. Currently, Congress is in a period of activity and expansion around the various programs that make up the workforce development system. Both the House and the Senate have been considering legislation that would change or eliminate a number of programs and services that comprise the current workforce development structure. As of fall 1995, the House of Representatives had passed the Consolidated and Reformed Education, Employment, and Rehabilitation Systems (CAREERS) Act and the Senate was on the verge on considering like-minded legislation. In addition to these legislative pieces, the 104th Congress was also considering welfare reform proposals and elimination of federal agencies including the Department of Education. The 104th Congress is likely to do the following:

Consolidate and eliminate programs. The various reports by the U.S. General Accounting Office counting the many programs with similar eligibility or activities were a clarion call for Congress and drive the current debate. The House and Senate legislation consolidates over ninety programs. The consolidation and elimination of programs will be replaced by block grants. The CAREERS Act has three block grants maintaining separate funding streams for adults, youth, and literacy programs. The Senate version gives states a single block grant, although amounts within that block grant may be designated for specific uses. In addition to changing funding, the consolidation and elimination of programs will also play out in changed requirements for the states and their relationship with federal government and local entities.

Develop a system that provides customer choice and easy access to services. The underlying principle is that consumers of services should have the opportunity to be more involved in their workforce preparation. Both the House and the Senate legislation allow the use of vouchers. With vouchers, individuals make their own choices about services needed and then, if they qualify, have the services paid for by the government through vouchers. However, in order for vouchers to be successful, information on education and training institutions needs to be collected so that customers can make informed choices. The legislative proposals and skills standards continue to shape our labor market information system.

Easier access to services may come through the development of one-stop centers. One-stop locations combine services in one place, giving customers easier access. One-stop as a concept is not limited to a physical location but may offer services electronically. As envisioned by Congress, each local workforce development board would develop the centers, which would be honest brokers by not providing services but only referring to existing community service providers.

Continue private sector involvement. The legislative proposals recognize that education and training programs must reflect the needs of business. Business has been involved in the existing programs through community boards. That involvement will be expanded through business participation on boards and the design of occupational training that meets business's needs. In both the House and Senate proposals, business will continue to be the majority of members of local boards, now named Workforce Development Boards. The Senate version also allows states to create a state workforce development board, a majority of whose members would represent business and industry. This board would design the state's workforce development programs. In addition, the Senate bill creates a National Workforce Development Board, also with a majority of business and industry members, to administer all federal responsibilities.

Provide maximum authority and responsibility to states and local communities. While Congress continues to call for accountability of workforce programs, the responsibility for accountability rests at the state level. States will set their own goals and performance measurements and report to the federal level. This follows the well-worn maxim that "one size does not fit all," meaning that the federal government is unable to require one outcome for the entire nation.

Although legislation provides specifics of how to fund populations or services, both the House and the Senate give the states flexibility in the expenditure of funds, allowing dollars to be transferred among block grants or funding streams. The states and localities will have further programmatic flexibility. For example, the Senate bill calls for a single comprehensive workforce development plan. This would replace the current system, in which each program develops its own plan, pretends to coordinate with other programs, and then ships the plan off to the federal government.

Create new and change current federal structures. The legislation now under consideration goes farther than previous efforts to build a workforce development system. The Senate bill would create a federal partnership to administer all federal responsibilities, including approval of state plans, negotiation of benchmarks with each state, and dissemination of best practices. The federal partnership would be managed by a governing board. Once the board is established, various divisions in the departments of Education and Labor would be eliminated.

However, some areas remain intractable to change. Both workforce development bills address the vocational rehabilitation system and try to bring them into the workforce development orbit. But although the House legislation changed vocational rehabilitation, it was stripped from the bill on the House floor, and the issue therefore died.

Other legislation pending in Congress would also change the subsystems of workforce development. Congress continues to debate where students will obtain college loans, whether from the educational institution or from banks. There also continues to be ongoing discussion about even the existence of the Department of Education.

These legislative proposals combined with reduced funding clearly will change the direction of workforce preparation in this country. The question that remains is whether with these changes we will truly have the wherewithal to develop a workforce development system either at the federal or at the state level.

Preparing for the Next Century

The real changes that will result from these structural and legislative alterations are impossible to predict. The merits and demerits will be debated throughout the country for some time to come. Regardless of the funding level, the organizational boxes, and the shifting roles of different levels of government, little progress will be made unless lessons learned from past and current efforts are incorporated into the implementation phase. There is a consistent set of lessons that have been gleaned from *across* several of the subsystems, such as youth employment and training programs and work/welfare. These lessons, many of which seem to be common sense, are seldom used to guide the efforts of federal or state policy makers.

The system and services should be client driven, not agency driven.

Services should be appropriate as to age and stage and should address the developmental needs of youth and adults.

The system should be based on knowledge and skill identified as needed to succeed in the global economy.

A successful program is one that is driven by a set of common goals and benchmarks of progress and achievement that are understood and used by all.

Continuous professional development of staffs is one of the best predictors of the success of any program.

Connecting work and learning throughout all phases of an individual's workforce preparation and retraining activities increases the chance that the individual will continue to pursue more education and increase his or her wages.

This rather short checklist reflects a very different way of doing business. It will require a strong national infrastructure that promotes best practice in the bringing together and development of leaders to manage the subsystems as well as the overall system.

Final Thoughts

It has been said that civilization is a sequence of new tasks. The challenges and opportunities in creating new forms of learning opportunities that will generate win-win results for students, employers, communities, and the state are substantial. The need for a national framework should be clear, one within which new forms of consortiums among the states, employer organizations, unions, colleges and universities, professional and trade associations, and other involved bodies can emerge. However, the real work for building the new system will occur within each state and its own local communities. The federal government is, in theory, giving them the tools to develop a workforce development system within their state. Whether they will be able to settle any or all of the questions and issues that have been raised in this chapter will only be known in time. Will enough time be allotted for the new paradigm to take hold? Will it be what we need to move into the twenty-first century?

References

American Youth Policy Forum. *Contract with America's Youth: Toward a National Youth Development Agenda.* Washington, D.C.: American Youth Policy Forum, 1994.

Carnevale, A. P., Gainer, L. J., and Meltzer, A. S. *Workplace Basics: The Essential Skills Employers Want.* San Francisco: Jossey-Bass, 1990.

Commission on the Skills of the American Workforce. *America's Choice: High Skills or Low Wages!* Rochester, N.Y.: National Center on Education and the Economy, 1990.

Goals 2000: Educate America Act. U.S. Public Law 103–227. Mar. 31, 1994.

Halperin, S. *School-to-Work: A Larger Vision.* Washington, D.C.: American Youth Policy Forum.

Hamilton, S. F., and Hamilton, M. A. *Opening Career Paths for Youth: What Can Be Done? Who Can Do It?* Washington, D.C.: American Youth Policy Forum.

Jobs for the Future. *Extending Employment and Training Policy to Adult Workers: Lessons from the CAEL Workforce Education Model.* Boston: Jobs for the Future.

Johnston, W. B., and Packer, A. H. *Workforce 2000: Work and Workers for the 21st Century.* Indianapolis, Ind.: Hudson Institute, 1987.

National Commission on Excellence in Education. *A Nation at Risk: The Imperative for Education Reform.* Washington, D.C.: U.S. Government Printing Office, 1983.

National Commission on Secondary Vocational Education. *The Unfinished Agenda: The Role of Vocational Education in High School.* Columbus, Ohio: National Center for Research in Vocational Education, 1984.

National Governors' Association. *Time for Results.* Washington, D.C.: National Governors' Association, 1986.

National Institute for Literacy. *Building State Performance Measurement, Reporting and Improvement Systems.* Washington, D.C.: National Institute for Literacy, 1995.

National Youth Employment Coalition. *Toward a National Youth Development System: How We Can Better Serve Youth at Risk.* Washington, D.C.: National Youth Employment Coalition, 1994.

Parnell, D. *The Neglected Majority.* Washington, D.C.: Community College Press, 1985.

William T. Grant Commission on Work, Family, and Citizenship. *The Forgotten Half: Non-College Youth in America.* Washington, D.C.: William T. Grant Commission on Work, Family, and Citizenship, 1988.

JOAN L. WILLS is director of the Center for Workforce Development of the Institute for Educational Leadership in Washington, D.C.

Academic institutions often lack an effective and economical means for evaluating learning that has taken place outside the college classroom. This chapter describes the American Council on Education assessment process and its outcome: college credit recommendations.

Awarding College Credit for Knowledge and Ability Gained Outside the College Classroom

Joan Schwartz, E. Nelson Swinerton

Today, more than ever, workforce participants are searching for ways to upgrade their skills and talents, often changing career paths in the process. As part of their change and growth, individuals have often taken workplace courses that have increased their knowledge and ability and have passed certification examinations that have provided them a means for demonstrating their knowledge and ability. These successfully completed courses and examinations can be applied to a college degree program.

Why Credit the Learning?

Each year, America's workforce—including both executive and technical personnel—update and improve their job-related knowledge and skills in company sponsored training. More and more are seeking access to further opportunity. Many of these workers seek to enhance their credentials by applying their workplace and distance learning training toward college and university degrees. Why are more skilled workers now seeking college degrees? There are five major reasons: competition in the global economy, a 59 percent change in technology every three years, the need for decision-making skills in all workers, corporate restructuring and resizing, and need for a North American world-class workforce.

This chapter is based on a paper presented at "Restricting Freedom? International Credit Transfer and Skill Recognition in the Late 20th Century," conference of the International Centre for Education in Development, University of Warwick at Coventry, England, July 4, 1995.

When employees bring their portfolios of workplace learning to colleges and universities for credit assessment on an individual basis, it becomes an expensive, time-consuming, and sometimes difficult procedure. All too often academic institutions lack an effective and economical means to accomplish these tasks. The American Council on Education (ACE) provides the link between the collegiate and noncollegiate system by relating workplace and distance learning training to college level courses and degree programs.

To encourage individuals to return to a postsecondary institution to gain the skills and learning they will need to participate in the global workforce of the twenty-first century, the educational community should assure the individuals that they will receive acknowledgment of the learning that they have already acquired. David Robertson argues that "individuals need to become *knowledge-rich;* that is, multi-proficient and self-mobilizing" (1995, p. 5). He sees the boundaries between institutions and society fading, with individuals getting and keeping proficiencies from many sources including universities, communities, and workplaces. In a report from the First Global Conference on Lifelong Learning, held in Rome in November 1994, Christopher Ball echoes this theme of developing human potential as fully as possible through lifelong learning: "This is because in the 21st century those individuals who do not practice lifelong learning will not work; those organizations which do not become learning organizations will not survive; those schools, colleges and universities which do not put their students first will not recruit" (1995, p. 8). He sees each individual taking the responsibility for putting together his or her own action plan. Institutional recognition of the learning gained from the individual, community, or workplace learning is an important part of this process.

Institutional recognition of nontraditional learning often encourages adults to attend, or return to, college or university to gain the needed knowledge for a skilled job and, in many cases, to earn a degree. Often, the acceptance of the credit provides the individual with confidence in his or her ability to achieve at the post secondary level. Acceptance of the credit for learning that has already taken place also enables the individual to complete the course of study more quickly and efficiently.

ACE provides an effective method for advancing the concept of the learning society. As the bridge between America's higher education institutions and the massive training and human resource development enterprise, ACE offers the potential for helping to enhance the quality and productivity of a substantially larger proportion of the workforce.

The process that the Center for Adult Learning and Educational Credentials (CALEC), the ACE office we represent, has developed for evaluating the learning acquired either through workplace courses offered by business, industry, labor unions, or government agencies, or through demonstration of learning by successful completion of national examinations or certification programs, affords an objective method of acknowledging competency-based learning. The process, which we will describe, reviews the course or examination content, and in the case of examinations, also looks at the examination's reliability and validity. The outcome of the review is college-level credit recommendations that can be applied to an individual's degree. Because the courses and the examinations are being reviewed, and not the individual who is taking the course or examination, the culture, race, and gender of the individual do not enter into the evaluation process. ACE has, in fact, evaluated courses and examinations that are offered internationally. For example, Learning Tree Inc. offers computer courses in various locations around the world, and the Institute for the Certification of Computer Professionals (ICCP) offers their four certification examinations in India, Pakistan, and various locations in the Far East.

Background

ACE is the major representative organization of higher education in the United States. Through its programs, activities, and policy-setting functions, it strives to ensure quality education and equal opportunity on the nation's campuses. Through its various divisions, ACE deals with a variety of postsecondary issues, such as the following: the Government Affairs office represents higher education before Congress; the Offices of Leadership Development and Minority Affairs promote the advancement of women and minorities to administrative positions within higher education; the Office of Policy Analysis and Research collects, monitors, and disseminates data needed for higher education policy making; and the Office of International Initiatives promotes international education on U.S. campuses, supports collaboration with institutions abroad, and participates in shaping U.S. policy relative to international education. CALEC promotes and encourages the adoption of policies by academic institutions that benefit adult learners by acknowledging nontraditional learning, that is, learning that has taken place outside the traditional college classroom, whether in the workplace, in the nontraditional classroom, or in the privacy of an individual's study.

CALEC has, for more than fifty years, served as a leader and catalyst in adult education. It has been in the forefront of assessing and credentialing learning acquired outside traditional educational institutions, validating the quality of learning, and promoting the recognition of this learning by educational institutions and other organizations.

Evaluation Process

In order to facilitate the acceptance of credit for nontraditional learning, ACE has developed evaluation processes that review courses and examinations on the basis of competency, or outcomes. The process for evaluating courses and examinations is basically the same, with review of credit by examination having a slightly different focus and an additional review team of psychometricians.

Organizations that have heard about our evaluation process and are interested in proceeding with a review approach the American Council on Education requesting an evaluation of their courses or examinations. Information about the review process, including costs and what materials the organization needs to provide the review team, is sent to the organization. The organization reads the information, gathers and prepares the needed materials, sends them to the Program Director for a preliminary review to confirm that the courses or examinations are eligible for the review process, and awaits final approval for a review.

Because organizations pay for the review, the ACE staff always reviews the materials beforehand to ensure that the materials are in order and that there is the possibility of some academic credit being recommended. If the submitted materials do not reflect the level of learning required for a credit recommendation, the materials are returned to the organization accompanied by an indication why a review is not feasible at that time. Recommendations for how to improve the materials for a credit review are usually included. This allows the organization to reconsider whether it wishes to have or to forgo a credit review.

Evaluating Workplace Learning

Once it receives and reviews the materials and determines that an evaluation is feasible, the ACE staff begins the process of bringing together an evaluation team of academic faculty that are experts in the fields covered by the courses or examination. Usually, the team consists of three faculty members with at least five years of teaching in their field of expertise, and an understanding, and appreciation of, nontraditional learning. The team consists of faculty from two-year and four-year institutions and, in some cases, from graduate-level institutions, depending on the course and examination content. The faculty is drawn from over three thousand academic institutions nationwide.

The evaluation date or dates are chosen (the number of days depends on the number of courses or examinations submitted for review), and the materials, the evaluators, and an ACE staff coordinator gather either at the organization or at the ACE offices in Washington, D.C. Often, the organization requesting the review will send all the materials to the evaluators before the review date. This premailing provides the individual evaluators time to review the materials before coming together with their colleagues to discuss the credit recommendations. The evaluators review all the materials submitted by the organization, gather on the appointed date(s), and discuss the amount and type of credit that should be recommended for the courses or examination.

The evaluators are briefed beforehand about what their task is during the evaluation. It is made clear to them that they are reviewing the materials to see whether the course or examination content is equivalent to what is currently being taught in the college or university classroom. Some questions that the evaluators ask are, Does this material overlap with what we are teaching? Does this material represent a complementary body of knowledge that would supplement what we are doing in the classroom and be worthy of credit? How could we best label this credit so that our colleagues in the field will understand the credit recommendation we are making? In all cases the team members must reach a consensus of opinion when determining the credit recommendation.

Often, there is no direct match between a particular course module that is being taught in the workplace or an examination used for certification and what is being taught in the college classroom. This is where the judgment and experience of the faculty play a crucial role in the determination of the college credit recommendation. The longer and broader the experience of the faculty on the review team is, the better and more accurate is their credit recommendation. What the faculty are looking for are the competencies that are gained through passing the course or examination. The faculty reviewers can then compare these competencies, or outcomes, to those gained through the college courses taught by the faculty reviewers. This is the common link between the nontraditional and the traditional learning.

There is no organizational representation during the actual review process. The representatives only meet with the team members to provide a short introduction to their organization's program, including facts and figures, and to provide an opportunity for the evaluators to ask any questions that have arisen during their review of the materials. After the initial introduction and the question and answer period, the representatives leave the review room, and they do not meet the review team again until the end of the review. At that time the team members present the organization's representatives with the final results of their review including the credit recommendations.

This is usually the best time for the organization's representatives to ask questions about the amount or labeling of the credit recommendations. Since the evaluation team can come from various parts of the country, this is the one time when all evaluators are together and available for questions. There are other opportunities during the next few weeks when the organization can raise questions about the credit recommendations and their labeling, but the logistics of discussion are not as simple.

The preceding description of a course evaluation also pertains to the ACE examination review conducted by the Credit by Examination Program. Although the procedure is similar, examinations also receive a review by a team of psychometricians. This team is tasked with reviewing the examinations from a technical psychometrical viewpoint. The questions they ask about the examination include the following: Is this examination reliable and valid? Is there sufficient examination security? Are the test items current and up to date? Is the cut score valid? How many classes would my students have to successfully complete to pass this examination? Does passing the test reflect the level of competency equal to that of my students?

In reviewing the examinations, the main goal of the reviewers is to determine the level of competency demonstrated by the individual. When or where the individual learned what is being tested is unimportant; how long the examinee took to learn the material is unimportant; what is important is whether the student has mastered a body of knowledge and ability and can demonstrate that knowledge and ability through the examination—and to a level that reflects a depth of knowledge taught in a college classroom.

During the review of a course or examination, not only is a credit recommendation decided upon, but a detailed description of the course or examination is produced by the faculty reviewers. They write a detailed description of the course or examination goals, outcomes, and content, including the final credit recommendations. The examination exhibit also includes a report by the technical team including information on the test's reliability and validity. The above information usually provides the academic institution with sufficient information to make a credit award.

The final step in the review process is for the ACE staff to mail the final report to the organization's representative for publication in organizational newsletters and local newspapers. Also, ACE encourages the organizations to inform the individuals who have successfully completed the course or examination about the availability of the credit recommendations. ACE publishes the evaluation results in their semiannual newsletter, and ultimately they are printed in the appropriate *Guide to Educational Credit by Examination*. The *Guide* is published yearly and is sold to colleges and universities (see the resource list at the end of the chapter).

Awarding Credit Recommendations

The ACE Center for Adult Learning recommends that colleges and universities accept the credit recommendations toward an individual's degree program. The ACE evaluation programs described above are designed to facilitate the acceptance of the credit for extra-institutional learning. Many American academic institutions do not have the faculty or inclination to take on an evaluation of an individual's nontraditional learning; by conducting the evaluations, ACE saves the college the time and expense of an evaluation and provides the individual with a head start in earning credit for learning already acquired. The process described above is acceptable to the academic officials, and over the years they have had a sufficient number of students transferring ACE college level credit to know that the credit recommendations are a valid indicator of learning. The academic officials trust ACE and its work.

As part of its service, ACE provides evaluated organizations with access to the Registry of Credit Recommendations: a record-keeping system that provides individuals with a permanent computerized document that allows them to easily retrieve their ACE credit recommendations. The document is in a format familiar to American college officials and includes the seal of the American Council on Education.

Of course, the final decision about acceptance of the ACE credit recommendations rests with the academic institutions. The acceptance of the credit is usually determined by a number of factors: the mission and goals of the academic institution, its policies and procedures for accepting nontraditional credit, the program of study the individual is pursuing, and whether there is duplication with other transfer credit being applied to the individual's degree plan.

If individuals are attending an institution that caters to adult learners, and they are not transferring courses from other institutions, then there is a good chance that much of the nontraditional learning may be accepted toward their degree programs. If, on the other hand, students complete an ACE-evaluated course or examination and they are near completion of their academic program, it is less likely that the ACE credit will be accepted. ACE encourages individuals to request application of their credit recommendations early in their academic program, whenever possible.

Various surveys done over the last five to seven years indicate that colleges award, on average, twelve to fourteen semester hours of ACE credit recommendations. For adults attending college for the first time, or as returning students, this amount of credit provides a savings in time and money, as well as offers a boost to their self-confidence; after all, they have proven to themselves that they can successfully complete college-level work.

Implications

What social and economic implications does recognition of nontraditional learning have for the individual and the society at large? Many. The recognition of nontraditional learning often begins the process of an individual thinking about and ultimately attending college. Anecdotal information indicates that after deciding to attend college, many individuals discover they like going to classes, that they like studying subjects they never previously thought about, and that they want to graduate from college more to meet their own personal goals than to increase their job opportunities. Surely, career advancement is a strong motivator, but not necessarily the major motivator.

Studies show that learning is addictive; students are more prone to become lifelong learners and continue to "pop in" to academe to gain more education whenever they feel the need. It is assumed that these individuals will more easily adapt to changing situations in the workforce—that they will be ongoing, productive members of society. Also, they have a strong influence on their children. Studies show that children of parents attending school will take a greater interest in school, will have a lower dropout rate, and will continue with their education and attend college.

Opportunities in the twenty-first century will belong to the individuals and the nations that develop a well-educated and skilled workforce. Lifelong learning will be a requirement, not a choice. A well-educated workforce will reflect a society that can be flexible and cope with constant change. Movement within the global workforce will become easier; because individuals' skills are definable in terms of competencies, they can move about the international labor market, able to have any business organization quickly assess whether their skills and learning are applicable to the job requirements of the organization. For example, L. Otala observes: "Employee mobility is increasing in

Europe with its newly open labor market and may grow even more in the U.S. with defense conversion programs" (1993, p. 27). He notes that the globalization of business makes it possible for engineers to move from one country to another. He says, "Mobility increases the need to grant credit for all studies and ensure that credit is transferable" (p. 27).

There will be no room in the global workforce for prejudice with regard to race, ethnicity, or gender. The desire for a skilled workforce will compel the employer to view potential employees in terms of their skills and competencies and how they can best meet the organization's needs. Hiring will become "colorblind" out of necessity. Individuals who view learning as part of their total life pattern will benefit and will help bring about the diverse and multicultural society of the twenty-first century.

References

Ball, C. "Findings." In *Lifelong Learning—Developing Human Potential: An Action Agenda for Lifelong Learning for the 21st Century.* Report from the First Annual Conference on Lifelong Learning, Rome, 1994. Brussels, Belgium: World Initiative on Lifelong Learning, 1995.

Otala, L. "Studying for the Future." *ASEEE PRISM,* Oct. 1993.

Robertson, D. "The Globalisation of Choice and Mobility: International Policies, and Frameworks for Flexibility in Lifetime Learning." Paper presented at "Restricting Freedom? International Credit Transfer and Skill Recognition in the Late 20th Century," conference of the International Centre for Education in Development, University of Warwick at Coventry, England, July 4, 1995.

JOAN SCHWARTZ is director of the Credit by Examination Program at the American Council on Education, Washington, D.C.

E. NELSON SWINERTON is director of the American Council on Education/Program on Noncollegiate Sponsored Instruction at the American Council on Education, Washington, D.C.

An overview of experiential learning programs developed for adult students in colleges and universities is presented, along with issues, noteworthy programs, and suggestions for improving practices.

Experiential Learning in the Workplace

Iris M. Saltiel

> The trouble with using experience as a guide is that the final exam often comes first and then the lesson.
>
> —Anonymous

Today's workforce needs to be better educated and more highly skilled than yesterday's. Career path employment opportunities for those with limited education and without college credit have decreased and continue to do so (Carnevale, Gainer, and Meltzer, 1988). Many who are already employed are responding to their employer's changing demands for college credentials. Employees without academic credentials are scrambling as they seek out colleges and universities to obtain a degree.

In the workplace and in colleges and universities, the use of experiential learning is growing. Employees often seek out colleges and universities that offer an opportunity to utilize experiential learning as part of earning a degree. This chapter is concerned with prior learning assessment. It begins with an overview of the evolution of experiential learning programs, gives examples of experiential learning programs, presents issues concerning experiential learning in the workplace, provides illustrations of experiential learning in workplace programs, and concludes with suggestions for improving practices.

Evolution of Experiential Learning Programs

In the early 1970s a Carnegie Commission report called for the development of opportunities for adults to earn degrees without attending classes. Consequently,

NEW DIRECTIONS FOR ADULT AND CONTINUING EDUCATION, no. 68, Winter 1995 © Jossey-Bass Publishers

colleges such as Thomas Edison State College, Charter Oak, Regents, the State University of New York, and the Union Institute developed to serve the needs of adult learners. Shortly after, many colleges along with the Educational Testing Service founded the Council for Adult and Experiential Learning (CAEL) to "conduct valid, reliable assessments of learning acquired outside institutions" (Lamdin, 1992, p. 67).

Colleges working with the American Council of Education (ACE) and through professional associations that serve adult learners, such as the American Association for Adult and Continuing Education (AAACE), the Association for Continuing Higher Education (ACHE), CAEL, the National University Continuing Education Association (NUCEA), Coalition of Adult Education Organizations (CAEO), and the College Board, have accomplished much in the last twenty years to assist adults going to college. Through their collective efforts a great deal of programming was developed to serve adults who want or need to further their education. The successes of their efforts have in no small part contributed to the growing agreement of college administrators with Simerly's (1991) statement: "The adult student who works full-time and attends school part-time has become the 'new majority' for higher education" (p. 6). In fact, these students currently make up 44 percent of the undergraduate population (U.S. Bureau of Census, 1992). A natural extension of this phenomenon has been colleges conducting classes and other student services, such as on-site advising and course registration, at corporations and organizational sites.

Experiential Learning

Experiential learning is based on Dewey's philosophical belief that direct experience is essential to learning (1938). For Dewey (1938, p. 25), "All genuine education comes about through experience." Lamdin connects experiential learning to academic pursuits: experiential learning is "any learning in which the learner is in direct touch with the realities being studied" (p. 68). And according to McCormick (1990), "Experiential learning is like learning about roller coasters while buckled into the front car. The learning is more exciting, deeper, and richer; because of this, students are more likely to recall it" (p. 27). So one can see that learning is enhanced by experience. For the employed adult learner the need for experience-based learning is even more necessary. The classroom-based learning model is not as effective with the working adult, whose day-to-day life is far more compelling and requires active wrangling with problems in "real life working situations."

In higher education, the use of experiential learning allows students to earn college credit by demonstrating the knowledge they already have. It is not uncommon for working adult students to have acquired college-level knowledge without being in the classroom. As a result, the development of methods and standards to assess knowledge in a particular domain are often a feature of adult-centered degree programs. Most colleges offering experientially based programming require that courses consist of both validation of prior knowledge and instruction. Instruction occurs when the learner decides to acquire new knowledge. The movement has grown to encompass both validation of prior learning and instruction of knowledge. A critical aspect of this validation, in fact, is that it must be done course by course. A student is expected to demonstrate knowledge and expertise in a particular course.

An experiential learning program can also be structured only for the purpose of assessing knowledge gained prior to an individual's current collegiate experience. Essentially, adult students may have already learned a great deal in highly specific content areas. Students who can document and demonstrate their learning can receive college credit. Over one thousand colleges nationally allow adult students to use prior experiential learning to earn college-level credit for demonstrated learning (McCormick, 1990). Given the adult student's practical problem-solving approach when considering paths to earning an educational credential, they will often select a college on the basis of their ability to use experiential learning in the degree program (Lamdin, 1992).

Prior Learning Assessment

Prior experiential learning is often called prior learning assessment or portfolio assessment at colleges and universities. The term *prior learning assessment* is used to encompass the options adult students use to earn credit for knowledge they already have. Students often will use a variety of assessment methods, including the following:

Testing or credit by examination, such as that administered by the College-Level Examination Program (CLEP).

Portfolio assessment, which allows students to demonstrate college-level knowledge through written documents or products on a course-by-course basis judged through college course descriptions from regionally accredited colleges.

The Program on Noncollegiate Sponsored Instruction (PONSI), a program of the American Council on Education (ACE), in which courses taken through business, industry, labor unions, and other noncollegiate providers have been evaluated toward an academic credit recommendation; this is described by Schwartz and Swinerton in the previous chapter.

Military training, which has also been evaluated by ACE; many students who have been in the military are able to earn substantial college credit for their experience and training.

Testing and portfolio assessment are individual assessment procedures for awarding academic credit for learning, while PONSI and military evaluations are organizational processes.

Issues Concerning Experiential Learning in the Workplace

The issues concerning experiential learning in the workplace are complicating its use in higher education. In the following, four issues surrounding experiential learning that affect the collegiate experience of adult learners are identified and explained.

Experiential Learning Is Still Controversial. On an individual basis, colleges and universities have always provided the means for students who seek a way to earn advanced placement in their pursuit of a degree. Sometimes it has been through credit by examination; other times an individual professor, typically the chairperson of the department, would assess a student to determine if the student holds sufficient knowledge to skip the introductory course and be placed into a more advanced course. This decision has always been made by departmental faculty on a case-by-case basis.

The use of experiential learning as an integral part of a college program represents an institutional belief that college-level learning can and does occur in noncollegiate settings. Mission statements and policies that govern the institution endorse their commitment. Institutions that truly espouse experiential learning and assessment have been regarded as innovative by some and "diploma mills" by others (ACE/CALEC/The Alliance, 1990). Almost a quarter of a century has passed since many were started, yet they are still regarded as the cutting edge of higher education and "risque."

Standards in Prior Learning Assessment. Nightmares surround college prior learning administrators when they hear stories about the student who was awarded ninety-five semester hours for twenty years of work experience. They have all experienced prospective students who have shown them a résumé and asked, "How much credit can I get?" Fortunately, prior learning assessment procedures that meet the principles of good practice as outlined by Urban Whitaker in his book *Assessing Learning: Standards, Principles and Procedures* (1989) are followed by most colleges and universities today. Thomas Edison State College, a pioneer in this field, holds an annual Institute on Prior Learning Assessment to assist colleges and universities in the nuts and bolts of portfolio assessment programs.

Another accepted way in which students demonstrate college-level knowledge in subject areas commonly taught in college classrooms is equivalency testing. Students earn credit by documenting their college-level knowledge and skills on an examination. These examinations typically consist of a number of questions in a multiple-choice format that meet test construction standards of reliability and validity. Over four hundred college-level examinations are offered in a variety of subjects and through different testing programs.

The most commonly known program is the College Board's CLEP. Other testing programs commonly used by working adult students include the Thomas Edison College Examination Program, the American College Testing Proficiency Examination Program, DANTES (originally designed for military personnel), the Ohio University Examination Program, and the New York University Proficiency Testing in Foreign Language Program. All of these programs reflect the awareness of the corporate adult student as a significant segment of the college-going population as well as provide for the specific needs of the corporate employee and employer.

Translating Training into Education. Training does not automatically translate to education. Corporations view training and education as "investments" in their workforce (Eurich, 1990). Although the terms *training* and *education* are often used interchangeably, there is a difference. Training is geared to the achievement of the organizational goal and to helping employees improve their performance on their current job (Darkenwald and Merriam, 1982). "Education prepares the employee for a place in the organization different from the one now held" (Nadler in Darkenwald and Merriam, 1982, p. 65). It is a "deliberate, systematic, and sustained effort to transmit, evoke, or acquire knowledge, attitudes, values, or skills" (Darkenwald and Merriam, 1982, p. 6). While both training and education aim to transmit knowledge, the differences can be extreme. The two often have incompatible missions, intents, philosophies, and resources. When combined thoughtfully and deliberately, the partnership is powerful.

Corporations often combine resources for training and education (Carnevale, Gainer, and Villet, 1990; Eurich, 1985). Business and industry invest $60 billion annually to provide formal education and training for their workforce (Eurich, 1990). This undoubtedly is one of the factors that contributes to the interactive nature of training and education. Training that has been evaluated for academic credit through ACE's PONSI is used by employees to meet degree requirements at over 1,500 colleges throughout the United States. Some colleges have even designed degree programs around ACE evaluations to meet a particular corporate need.

Formal education is frequently reimbursed by employer tuition aid programs. At least 85 percent of United States companies currently have tuition aid plans (Eurich, 1990). This investment will allow corporations to have a highly skilled and qualified workforce during this next decade. How well a workforce can adapt to changing requirements and demands contributes to a company's survival.

College Bureaucracies. Aslanian and Brickell (1988) identified "logistical ease" among the services that adults desire most in a college. Being able to park, locating classrooms, and finding the bookstore open all help to create a positive climate for learners. However, in many colleges credit for prior learning use is complicated by conflicting policies regarding what qualifies as "prior learning" versus "transfer in credit" and in which areas of a degree program these different types of learning can be used.

When colleges design degree programs specifically for working professionals, policies must be developed that explain how and where experiential learning fits into the degree program. Davis (1994) explains, "The institution should take care in determining the fit of this learning into the student's degree program, considering the components of the degree, the currency of the learning, and whether it builds on or duplicates knowledge for which the student already has received credit" (p. 19). Often a college will develop a program for a particular corporation. The college will sometimes conduct an on-site review of the courses, materials, and course instructors in addition to or in lieu of a PONSI review. The college faculty will then determine which company courses will be accepted and where they fit into the degree program. There are many ways that colleges and associations have designed educational programs building on PONSI evaluations to assist employees to earn academic credentials.

Noteworthy Experiential Learning Programs for Working Adults

CAEL has been known for development and coordination of prior learning assessment strategies across college and business sectors. These strategies include academic and administrative standards based upon policies for quality assurance and best practices (Whitaker, 1989). CAEL has also created educational programs that utilize experiential learning for working adults, with employers, unions, employees, and educational providers all working together through CAEL's joint ventures concept (CAEL, 1992).

One program developed by the College Board for organizations to extend the use of credit by examination by working adults is called Corporate CLEP. Corporate CLEP includes CLEP material to disseminate to employees, as well as offering employees an opportunity to participate in career and educational planning through its Corporate Counselor materials (College Board, 1994). This program is designed to meet the specific needs of the corporate employee and employer.

Thomas Edison State College, which was founded in 1972 by the New Jersey Board of Higher Education to provide "diverse and alternative methods of achieving a collegiate education of the highest quality for mature adults" (Thomas Edison State College 1995–97 catalogue, p. 4), currently has over nine thousand students and more than eleven thousand graduates worldwide. Thomas Edison students develop their own degree completion program using a variety of credit earning methods and aided by an adviser who takes into account the students' timeline, degree requirements, and personal learning preferences. Students work with the college's staff by telephone, fax, and mail, in person, and electronically through the Computer Assisted Lifelong Learning Network to complete degree requirements. Through the various programs and initiatives, working adults are able to utilize their accumulated knowledge through their work and life experiences to earn credit toward an academic degree.

The Weekend College at the College of Saint Elizabeth, also in New Jersey, provides an example of a burgeoning form of college programming for adult students. The Weekend College program was designed "to extend educational opportunities to highly motivated men and women who work full time" (Weekend College of Saint Elizabeth 1992–93 catalogue) to earn an undergraduate degree. The Weekend College allows students to earn twenty-four or more credits a year over three semesters and summer school sessions. Each course meets every other week over the semester with the remaining class time designated as Conference Review Time with the professor. The college has been in existence for seventeen years and has several thousand graduates. Over five hundred students are currently enrolled in this program.

Salem County College, in New Jersey, provides another example of a degree program designed specifically for a company. Its associate degree in nuclear engineering was developed specifically for workers of Public Service Electric and Gas Company. The company provides support to the college for the running of the program, and many of the courses are taught at company locations. Many company courses are offered for academic credit through the college. Support services from Salem County College, such as registration for courses and academic advisement, are available at company locations.

Suggestions for Improving Practice

In conclusion, I offer the following suggestions for colleges and universities that seek to integrate experiential learning into their programs.

Provide technical assistance. Experiential learning can be a complex concept to comprehend and interpret for others. Work with the organizational liaison to help the organization learn more about prior experiential learning and collegiate programs. One successful strategy used by Thomas Edison College that started serendipitously is to have the organizational liaison also be a student of the college. In addition, invest the time to understand the conceptual framework and appropriate usages when working with a corporation or organizational entity.

Conduct a needs assessment. In Jane Vella's (1994) *Learning to Listen, Learning to Teach,* she cites Thomas Hutchinson (1978) on the subject of needs assessment: "Who needs what as defined by whom? The WWW question . . ." (p. 4). Take into consideration the needs of the client (population to be served), the organizational needs (sponsoring corporation or agency), and the college's ability to provide the services.

Conclusion

The use of experiential learning in the workplace is a vibrant component of earning a degree for adult students. The strategies working students have employed as a way to earn their degrees are representative of the policy shifts American higher education has made to recognize the wealth of knowledge adult students hold. As technology advances, we will see more workers seeking out colleges and universities that offer an opportunity to utilize experiential learning as part of earning a degree in ways we have not yet developed.

References

American Council on Education Center for Adult Learning and Educational Credentials/The Alliance. *Principles of Good Practice for Alternative and External Degree Programs for Adults.* Washington, D.C.: American Council on Education Center for Adult Learning and Educational Credentials/The Alliance, 1990.

Aslanian, C. B., and Brickell, H. M. *How Americans in Transition Study for College Credit.* New York: College Entrance Examination Board, 1988.

Carnevale, A. P., Gainer, L. J., and Meltzer, A. S. *Workplace Basics: The Skills Employers Want.* American Society for Training and Development. Washington, D.C.: U.S. Department of Labor, 1988.

Carnevale, A. P., Gainer, L. J., and Villet, J. *Training in America: The Organization and Strategic Role of Training.* San Francisco: Jossey-Bass, 1990.

College Board. *Corporate CLEP Fact Sheet.* New York: College Board, 1994.

Council for Adult and Experiential Learning. *Closing the Skills Gap: New Solutions.* Chicago: Council for Adult and Experiential Learning, 1992.

Darkenwald, G. G., and Merriam, S. B. *Adult Education: Foundations of Practice.* New York: HarperCollins, 1982.

Davis, L. H. "Relating Work to Adult Higher Education." *Journal of Continuing Higher Education,* 1994, 42 (1), 17–22.

Dewey, J. *Experience and Education.* New York: Collier, 1938.

Eurich, N. P. *Corporate Classrooms: The Learning Business.* Princeton, N.J.: Carnegie Foundation for the Advancement of Teaching, 1985.

Eurich, N. P. *The Learning Industry: Education for Adult Workers.* Princeton, N.J.: Carnegie Foundation for the Advancement of Teaching, 1990.

Hutchinson, T. "Community Needs Analysis Methodology." Unpublished paper, University of Massachusetts, 1978.

Lamdin, L. *Earn College Credit for What You Know.* (2nd ed.) Chicago: Council for Adult and Experiential Learning, 1992.

McCormick, D. W. "The Painful Emotions of Prior Experiential Learning Assessment." *Adult Learning,* 1990, 2 (2), 26–28.

Simerly, R. G. "Preparing for the 21st Century: Ten Critical Issues for Continuing Educators." *Journal of Continuing Higher Education,* 1991, 39 (2), 2–12.

U.S. Bureau of the Census. *School Enrollments—Social and Economic Characteristics of Students: 1990.* Current Population Reports. Washington, D.C.: U.S. Government Printing Office, 1992.

Vella, J. *Learning to Listen, Learning to Teach: The Power of Dialogue in Educating Adults.* San Francisco: Jossey-Bass, 1994.

Whitaker, U. *Assessing Learning: Standards, Principles, and Procedures.* Philadelphia: Council for Adult and Experiential Learning, 1989.

IRIS M. SALTIEL *is director of enrollment services at Thomas Edison State College, Trenton, N.J.*

*The changing workplace of the future will require the development of
new paradigms for the professional preparation and career
development of workplace educators.*

Preparing Workplace Learning Professionals

W. Franklin Spikes

In order to succeed in the modern workplace, today's employees are being
required to learn new skills and adopt new patterns of behavior ("The New
World of Work," 1994; Gill, 1995). The movement toward total quality management, service-driven, team-oriented, globally competitive organizations in
which the traditional role of management has been redefined to better fit current business paradigms is at the root of the need for the development of these
new skills. Many workplace education, training, and development initiatives
have also been undertaken in an attempt to keep up with the learning-related
demands of today's organizations. (Carnevale and Carnevale, 1994). Carnevale,
Gainer, and Meltzer (1989), among others, have written extensively about the
need to rethink both how we prepare people for their initial entry into the
workplace and how we develop those competencies required to sustain high
levels of productivity by existing members of the workforce. They have stressed
the need for the development of increased skills in communication, problem
solving, creative thinking, computation, and learning how to learn (Carnevale,
Gainer, and Meltzer, 1989). With this increased interest has come such recent
federal initiatives as the school-to-work transition program and displaced
worker training projects, which have attempted to provide alternative mechanisms for acquisition of new skills by first-time employees and workers without jobs. In a related initiative, the American College Testing Service has
developed the Work Skills Program, a job profiling and testing endeavor that
is designed to diagnose existing job skills and match these skills with the specific ones that are needed on a variety of jobs.

   Given the rather broad interest that has recently been focused upon the
development of a workforce that possesses a new and expanded skill set, it

would seem logical that an equal effort would be taking place to identify the skills needed by and to train the trainers, educators, and facilitators of workplace learning programs in a comparable way. However, an examination of current practice indicates that this is not the always the case. Accordingly this chapter will examine several issues related to preparing workplace educators for the new and competitive business environment that they face now and will face in the years ahead. For example, what must workplace educators know or do differently today than they have in the past to remain proficient in their jobs? How must their initial and ongoing preparation differ from that which they have received in years past? And what modifications to existing delivery systems should be made in order to better accommodate the new needs of today's and tomorrow's corporate educator?

Three Types of Workplace Educators

Workplace educators come to their profession from a number of different fields and possess different levels of professional preparation. One of the more traditional models used to prepare workplace educators is the "coach to principal" approach that has historically taken place in many of the nation's public schools. Here an outstanding coach of football, basketball, or almost any other sport is moved into a major administrative role not because of his or her success at or training in public school administration but because of success on the athletic field. It is assumed that the role of coach equates favorably with the role of principal. The thinking here seems to follow the lines that if one can manage a football team and win, one can certainly effectively administer a school, direct the activities of its staff, and provide a positive learning climate for young people. The workplace corollary to this practice has been to promote the sales manager (or production, operations, or other type of manager) to the role of trainer, workplace educator, or training manager. As in the coach-to-principal transition, the sales manager to sales trainer model assumes that success in the sales field naturally provides the skill set necessary to be an equally skilled sales educator or trainer. It is assumed that the same skills that have led to sales success will transfer to the workplace learning arena. Often in organizations that use this model, managers find themselves in the situation of being a field manager on Friday and a trainer with a full training load on the next Monday. Advocates of this model argue that it is clearly better to employ trainers that have high levels of product, operations, or systems knowledge and develop their training competencies later than it is to do the reverse. Subject-matter expertise is clearly valued more highly in this model than knowledge about the adult learning process, instructional design skills, or training competencies. Sadly, in organizations that use this approach, training and workplace education programs are peppered with the "war stories" of the trainer. More often than not, the opportunity to use what is known both about how adults learn and the manner in which effective instruction of adults can be implemented is overlooked. Education and training-related professional development activities frequently do not occur in these organizations because of the high classroom training load that is carried by the newly appointed trainer.

A spin-off of this model is the one that recognizes that there is value in trainers having preparation in some educational field. In organizations that have this view, having product or operational knowledge or success is viewed as being important, but teaching experience and skill are seen as being no less important. Organizations holding these ideas have adopted the "any teaching experience is better than no teaching experience" perspective. Here workplace educators typically have public school teaching backgrounds. In these instances subject matter expertise is generally considered to be of little importance. Product knowledge is thought to be something that can be developed through on-the-job training interventions. Problematically, though, in environments such as that of the public school, the organizational value system, the subject matter, and the learners differ markedly from those found in the workplace. Without experience in teaching and working with adult learners, and without understanding the nature of the business environment, with its focus on profitability, workplace educators who have come from a public school background are often substantially handicapped in performing their new role.

With the advent of graduate programs in adult and continuing education and in human resource development has come yet a third model for preparing workplace educators. Formal preparation in the field at the masters and doctoral degree levels is available at numerous universities throughout North America. Initially, graduate work in the field of adult and continuing education was thought by many to be the best alternative to employ in overcoming many of the inherent weaknesses found in the "promote the coach to principal" and the "any teacher is better than no teacher" approaches of the past. Curricular recommendations for such programs were promulgated by the Commission of Professors of Adult Education (Zeph, 1991). Among other things, graduate students in adult education were provided information about adult learning and development, program planning and evaluation, and the social and psychological foundations of the field.

With the rise of interest in the field of human resource development has come similar opportunities for advanced study. In these programs a greater focus is placed on training, organizational development, consulting, and instructional design. Often graduate study in human resource development also places some emphasis upon some of the traditional personnel-related business functions of wage and salary administration, benefit management, and labor and employee relations.

Graduate study in both adult education and human resource development has provided the basis for workplace educators to enter their field with a greater understanding of routine business practices and the issues surrounding adult learning and development. Often, however, graduates of these programs experience a situation in which because of the nature of the academic enterprise, integrated learning that is drawn from the best and most appropriate elements of both fields does not occur. Similarly, the university faculty members teaching in these programs often were themselves trained at a time when workplace education did not have the prominence that it has today. Thus they, like their students, may well be lacking in current business-related experience or may be teaching from a perspective developed when graduate study in human resource development was not as prominent or substantial as it is today. Clearly knowledge of and experience with traditional adult education endeavors such as adult basic education programs, college and university continuing education programs, and social justice initiatives is important and useful in preparing educators to work in these specialized areas of practice. However, it is equally true that workplace educators must have the same type of opportunity to learn from faculty members with specialization in workplace learning practices. The dilemma that is posed by the current manner in which workplace educators obtain these jobs, the nature of the professional preparation that they may (or may not) have received, and the changing nature of the skills required in today's workplace is a complex one. What alternatives exist then to address this situation? Can an educational model be created that will help workplace educators achieve a better sense of alignment between the demands of the workplace and their education preparation and experiential background?

Three-Phase Approach to Preparing Workplace Educators

With the changing nature of the workplace in the years ahead, workplace educators of the future are going to require new skills that in many ways are far different from those that their current counterparts possess. The models of education and job attainment used today will no longer be appropriate for meeting the educational demands of tomorrow. Likewise, no one field of study, be it adult and continuing education, human resource development, or business administration, will corner the market in preparing educators to enter workplace roles. Similarly, professional preparation of workplace educators can no longer be confined to either a graduate program on a university campus or to on-the-job training in the workplace. Rather, integrated, multidisciplinary field-based and campus-based educational initiatives must be put in place that will provide learning opportunities throughout the professional life of the workplace learning professional. For this to occur, the professional preparation of workplace educators must be thought of as being a lifelong enterprise that, when viewed as a learning continuum, is divided into three distinct yet interrelated phases. Key elements of the model will be discussed below.

Phase 1: Initial Professional Preparation and Exploration. Phase 1 of this continuum consists of activities related to the initial training and career exploration of the workplace educator. Opportunities for the workplace educator of the future are provided so that the learner can explore a wide variety of roles (McLagan, 1989). Field-based educational experiences should be provided for learners to become involved in various public and private-sector organizations under the direction of a master trainer or workplace educator. As in some of today's more progressive teacher education programs, formal faculty exchange relationships are developed between colleges and universities involved with the initial preparation of workplace educators and the field sites in which they do their work. Thus the development of workplace learning curricula, the means and methods of instruction to be utilized, and the evaluative procedures that will be used to measure student learning and success become the joint responsibility of field organizations and college and university professional development programs. In this phase workplace educators would also concentrate on the development of new skills needed by the workforce through engaging in multidisciplinary study of communications, modern management theory and practice, computational sciences, and problem solving and decision making along with foundations of learning, program development, and instructional design practices.

This phase would culminate in the learner receiving a baccalaureate degree and being provisionally prepared to enter his or her field of practice in an entry level position. In addition a workplace educator in this period of his or her career would initiate an individualized and self-directed professional development that would be ongoing and would serve to continuously refine and improve his or her skill set.

Phase 2: Advanced Preparation and Career Exploration. The second phase of this model focuses on the career exploration and advanced preparation of workplace educators. Here workplace educators focus on one specific area of interest or job role to be played. After a substantial period of employment in a workplace education program or with an organization that supports such initiatives, workplace educators in this second phase of their career can and should return to graduate-level study in a program that focuses on in-depth exploration of specific roles and functions among their work responsibilities. Advanced interdisciplinary study is emphasized. Substantial study of organizational development, adult learning and development, consulting, problem solving, applied research methodologies, and evaluative techniques should occur here. Opportunities for in-depth field experiences under the direction of a master workplace educator should be provided.

The development of expertise is focused more tightly here than in the exploratory period of Phase 1. Continuous learning activities should increase in Phase 2 as both the competencies and the job responsibilities of the workplace educator become more substantial. Here, too, on-the-job training becomes a more important element of the workplace educator's professional development. Mentoring should be encouraged for workplace educators at the advanced specialized level of their training. This phase will culminate in the workplace educator receiving a graduate degree, so the workplace educators at this advanced level will have developed the skills necessary to assume senior career leadership roles within their organization and profession and be prepared to move on to the third phase of the model, professional leadership and career redirection.

Phase 3: Professional Leadership and Career Redirection. Ideally, workplace learners who have mature careers in the field will have experienced significant administrative and managerial positions. They will hold advanced multidisciplinary degrees, they will have engaged in continuous self-directed learning programs, and they will have experienced meaningful episodes of on-the-job mentoring and career assistance. Their role in this last stage of their career development and preparation as a workplace educator shifts its focus from individual development to the development of their broadly based field of human resource development practice and the implementation of meaningful programs of leadership development of fellow practitioners. In this phase of the model, careful attention is also given to career redirection and exploration, to career reassessment and analysis, and to perhaps beginning a new role within their organization and field of practice. It is at this point that the development of leadership education initiatives such at those called for by Mason (1989) are implemented. Senior workplace learning specialists should also focus on postgraduate study that will further refine and focus their area of expertise and enable them to begin to make meaningful contributions to their profession through the development of significant research initiatives. They should also start to reexamine the issues important to the broadly defined field of workplace learning at this point in their professional lives and attempt to develop meaningful solutions to some of its more vexing and cutting-edge challenges. Similarly, it is through this process of research, reflection, and analysis that senior workplace educators will be given the opportunity to redirect their work and renew their careers in different and more challenging ways.

The Workplace Educator of Tomorrow

Ultimately the workplace educator of the twenty-first century is going to need to be someone who is be professionally adaptive and intellectually creative. Through personal and professional practices he or she is going to have to model what continuous learning and ongoing education can and does mean for the worker of the next generation. No longer can workplace educators be limited by the employment and educational practices of yesterday's and today's organization. No longer should coaches be promoted to principals and field managers to trainers. Neither can modern, creative, competitive organizations that value learning afford to hire workplace learning specialists who do not possess specific skills and knowledge related to facilitating adult learning in a for-profit environment.

It is an unproductive and meaningless exercise to continue to engage in the argument of whether graduate study in adult education or in human resource development is most appropriate for the initial or advanced professional preparation of workplace educators. Rather, perhaps a new paradigm for preparing workplace educators should be developed. Such a new paradigm should emphasize ongoing integrated learning over the life span of the employee; a combination of classroom-oriented, field-based, and on-the-job training; and lifelong professional development. It is only by ridding themselves of the myths of the past, shedding the old paradigms about their work and preparation, and adopting such new models as proposed here that workplace educators, like the organizations in which they are employed, will be able to operate in the ever more high-performance and globally competitive economy in which they will find themselves in the years ahead.

References

Carnevale, A. P., and Carnevale, E. S. "Growth Patterns in Workplace Training." *Training and Development,* May 1994, pp. 22–28.

Carnevale, A. P., Gainer, L. J., and Meltzer, A. S. *Workplace Basics: The Skills Employers Want.* Washington, D.C.: American Society for Training and Development and U.S. Department of Labor, 1989.

Gill, S. J. "Shifting Gears—High Performance." *Training and Development,* May 1995, pp. 25–31.

McLagan, P. A. *Models for HRD Practice.* Washington, D.C.: American Society for Training and Development, 1989.

Mason, R. C. "Developing Leaders in Institutions of Higher Education." In B. A. Quigley (ed.), *Fulfilling the Promise of Adult and Continuing Education.* New Directions for Continuing Education, no. 44. San Francisco: Jossey-Bass, 1989.

"The New World of Work." *Business Week,* Oct. 12, 1994, pp. 75–86.

Zeph, C. P. "Graduate Study as Professional Development." In R. G. Brockett (ed.), *Professional Development for Educators of Adults.* New Directions for Adult and Continuing Education, no. 51. San Francisco: Jossey-Bass, 1991.

W. FRANKLIN SPIKES is professor, Department of Foundations and Adult Education, College of Education, at Kansas State University in Manhattan.

*A collaborative, holistic, and integrated approach to workplace
education is needed to ensure success for organizations and individuals
in dealing not only with a complex, evolving workplace but with a
changing world.*

Workplace Basics in the 1990s: Critical Issues and Promising Practices

Sue Waugh Folinsbee

As we move into the next millennium, there is a pressing need to enhance skills such as reading, writing, math, and oral communication to deal with changing workplace needs. Changing technology, increased employee decision making, quality initiatives, and new government regulations have made workplace education a priority. A well-conceived training and development strategy attends to the basic skills needs of workers to ensure the successful attainment of short-term and long-term company goals. In the workplace, opportunities for basic skills development can provide the foundation for other learning.

Basic skills programs, like other workplace programs, tend to have a greater impact in workplaces that value employee input, encourage decision making, and promote ongoing learning. This type of workplace may provide an opportunity to plan and develop collaborative, holistic, integrated basic skills initiatives that will benefit both the individual and the organization.

The focus in this chapter is on collaborative workplace education, with the recognition that not all workplace environments are conducive to this kind of approach. In places that are not open to collaboration, other effective strategies for basic skills education can be used. For example, there are many successful union-based and union-led programs that provide basic skills education for their members with minimal or no company involvement.

Collaborative initiatives involve workers in program planning and decision making at every stage of development and work hard to marry individual and organizational needs. They respect and value the knowledge and experience that people individually and collectively bring, and are designed to assist people in developing new skills and self-confidence. These initiatives recognize that

NEW DIRECTIONS FOR ADULT AND CONTINUING EDUCATION, no. 68, Winter 1995 © Jossey-Bass Publishers

the workplace culture, communication systems, problems, and issues must be taken into consideration in order to ensure that expectations of education programs are realistic.

Some organizational policies and practices may limit the effectiveness of workplace programs. Changes to these policies and practices go hand in hand with learning opportunities for people at all levels of an organization. In addition, workplace basic skills programs are an integral part of a life-long learning continuum. A collaborative approach can provide opportunities for people to develop transferable skills they can use at work and in their communities.

I begin with a discussion of definitions of workplace basic skills. I then provide a brief North American perspective on the evolution of workplace learning that focuses on basics such as reading, writing, math, and oral communication. I follow this historical perspective with a discussion of some of the larger critical issues that can impede the long-term success of workplace initiatives. Last, I outline principles of good practice that speak to some of these issues.

Definitions and Evolving Terminology: Conceptualizing Workplace Literacy

Definitions and concepts of workplace literacy vary according to the philosophical orientations of the interest groups involved in establishing workplace programs. Common interest groups involved in workplace education include management, unions, workers, funders, and educational providers.

Definitions and Their Underlying Assumptions. Currently, there is a tension between the economic and social dimensions of workplace education. This tension is reflected in a narrow, job-related approach versus a broader one that emphasizes critical thinking and empowerment not only at the workplace but also in everyday life. To understand how these two approaches might represent different ends of a continuum, it is useful to look at four prevailing definitions of literacy originally developed by Susan Lytle at the University of Pennsylvania and fleshed out by Carol Young using a workplace context (Young, 1994). Definitions are important because they reflect underlying assumptions about workplace education that determine how one plans and implements educational programs and other strategies.

The four definitions describe literacy as (1) a set of skills such as reading and writing; (2) tasks, for example, taking minutes at a meeting; (3) social practices, which could include how teams communicate and make decisions; and (4) critical reflection and empowerment, through which people, individually and collectively, take action to address important issues. In definitions one and two, the focus is on the individual and the job task. The assumption is that the individual needs to change. In three and four, the focus is on the unit or the organization. The assumption is that systems need to change. I argue that both an organizational and an individual focus are needed for workplace basic skills initiatives that are integrated, holistic, and collaborative.

Young suggests that these definitions are not mutually exclusive; that the broadest and most inclusive definitions encircle the narrower definitions as in concentric circles. She identifies literacy as critical reflection and empowerment in keeping with high performance work organizations. Many workplace programs include activities that reflect all four definitions. The issue is not so much the activities reflected in actual programming but more importantly, what the underlying orientation of a workplace initiative is and who has determined it.

Terminology: Current Usage in the Field. I use *basic skills* interchangeably with other terms such as *workplace literacy* and *workplace education* to reflect current usage in the field.

Much of the terminology we use can be problematic (Folinsbee, 1995) not only in its underlying assumptions and congruency or lack of congruency with a particular ideology, but also in how different interest groups perceive these terms. For example, the term *literacy* is problematic because of the stigma it carries. Employees are reluctant to be associated with programs that carry this label. In addition, decision makers from both business and labor may interpret *literacy* narrowly and fail to recognize important needs within their organizations. On the other hand, using the word *literacy* ensures that the issue of adult basic education stays on the agenda of funders and policy makers. In addition, it carries a rich culture and history of experience that can contribute to the field of workplace education.

The term *basic skills* can be confused with the term entry-level skills. It can also be limiting because it is associated with a set of discrete abilities that are isolated from the broader social and political context of the workplace.

Workplace education is a more generic term coined by adult educators, and refers to learning that focuses on reading, writing, math, and oral communication. Although this expression seems more positive and inclusive, it can be confused with other kinds of training and education delivered at the workplace, and does not reflect changes to organizational policies and practices that may be needed. *Workplace development* is another expression that has been used to include basic skills, other educational initiatives, and changes to workplace systems (Folinsbee and Jurmo, 1994b). I will use these terms interchangeably, as appropriate.

A Historical Perspective

Adult basic education programs for the workplace have existed in the United States since the late sixties. For example, on-site adult basic education and high school equivalency programs were offered by companies and unions (Askov and Alderman, 1991). In Canada, English in the Workplace programs became prominent in the late seventies. These programs had a strong social and empowerment component, and many of them were run by organized labor.

Employee development programs with a focus on workplace basic skills came into vogue in the United States in the mid eighties and in Canada in the late eighties. In the United States the motivation was economic. Workplace programs to improve workers' basic skills were presented as the way to address new requirements, improve productivity, and enhance the country's competitive edge (Imel and Kerka, 1992; Shultz, 1992; U.S. Department of Labor and U.S. Department of Education, 1988).

In their review of the literature, Imel and Kerka found that since the mid eighties the focus has been on mastery of the basic skills aspects of specific job tasks determined by management. This is commonly known as the *functional context approach*. The National Workplace Literacy Program was set up in 1988 under the Adult Education Act to improve workers' literacy skills and to give the United States a competitive edge (U.S. Department of Education, 1992). The functional context approach has guided the National Workplace Literacy Program in developing the standards against which its funded programs are measured (Jurmo, 1994).

In Canada, workplace literacy gained prominence through the establishment of the National Literacy Secretariat (NLS) in 1988 by the federal government. The NLS's mandate is to involve all sectors of society, including business and labor, in creating a more literate Canada. In 1988, it began to fund workplace literacy projects emphasizing experimentation and innovation in what was a relatively new field.

In Canada, workplace literacy is recognized as both an economic and social issue because of a strong voice from labor and the literacy community, the mandate of the National Literacy Secretariat, and earlier English in the Workplace programs. In addition, work in Canada has been influenced by the Multicultural Workplace Program in Ontario, which began in the mid eighties and focused on an organizational analysis of workplaces. This program recognized that addressing communication and other issues in diverse workplaces needed to go beyond just language and basic skills programs for workers. In order to address these issues, it was essential to focus on all employees as potential participants for training as well as on organizational practices and policies.

This dual position of looking at workplace literacy as both a social and an economic issue was reinforced at a recent national workplace literacy policy conversation sponsored by the NLS (National Literacy Secretariat, 1995) which presented literacy not only as an economic issue but as a social, political, and cultural issue as well.

Emerging Trends in the Field

Imel and Kerka also noted in their review that several writers have challenged a narrow, job-related approach and notions linking workers' lack of literacy skills to economic decline. Several ethnographers have argued for a broader approach to workplace literacy that not only considers and values workers' input, existing skills, and knowledge but also emphasizes the larger workplace context (Darrah, 1991; Gowen, 1992; Hull, 1991; Young, 1994). They have found that an approach that focuses only on job-related tasks developed by management and outside experts does not reflect the needs of individuals or the complex ways in which people perform work. Nor does it develop the broad, transferable skills so important in today's shrinking job market. Stein (1990, p. 3) echoes the latter point when she asserts, "The demand for increased worker literacy skills that has emerged in the context of this reorganization of the workplace is, I will argue, a demand for broader literacy education rather than technocratic skill-building."

Imel and Kerka also found that more recently collaborative, participatory approaches are gaining prominence and that these approaches are aligned with the goals of high performance work organizations.

Since 1992, participatory approaches have continued to gain prominence and momentum. A collaborative approach (Folinsbee and Jurmo, 1994b) involves all interest groups in the planning and development of workplace initiatives. In a collaborative approach, workers and unions have real decision-making powers with respect to both the planning and outcomes of a basic skills initiative. A participatory approach to workplace education is reflected in recent publications of guidebooks in both countries; provincial and state policies insist on planning teams that include workers and a needs assessment before organizations receive funding. In addition, informal and formal gatherings across the continent among labor, management, practitioners, researchers, and funders who are committed to seeing a richer, more inclusive approach also suggest the trend outlined by Imel and Kerka.

Critical Issues

Several critical issues need to be tackled during this decade if we are to enrich and improve our practice and meet the needs of all interest groups.

Financial and Organizational Commitment to Training and Education. There is an inconsistency between the cry for a better educated and highly skilled workforce and the lack of investment in training and education by North American companies. In the United States, about 13 percent of employees participate in on-the-job training and most are not entry level employees. In addition, while workplace basic skills programs may be growing in large companies, smaller companies (nearly 99 percent of the rest of the businesses) cannot afford these programs (Shultz, 1992). In Canada, the National Training Survey (Canadian Labour Market and Productivity Centre, 1993) indicated that only 2 percent of training provided by Canadian companies was for basic skills. In a study with grocery products manufacturers, Doran (1995) found that companies cited basic skills as a priority but generally did not have concrete plans to implement such training.

More evidence needs to be provided to business and labor leaders to show them the value of workplace education that focuses on the basics. They need to see how skills like reading and writing can provide the foundation for other learning and are integral to workers' success in the changing workplace. This information is critical in motivating business and labor to get involved.

In-Depth and Comprehensive Evaluations of Workplace Programs. Evaluations for workplace basic skills programs have usually been carried out informally by instructors or outside evaluators. These evaluations may not provide enough accurate, in-depth, or relevant information (Sperazi and Jurmo, 1994). They may provide specific data about participant progress and attitudes toward programs but do not involve all the stakeholders in the planning of the evaluation strategy or provide information on outcomes affecting the workplace.

In-depth information about the expected and unexpected outcomes of workplace programs provides evidence for the continued financial investment in current programs. It also provides evidence that can assist others in making informed decisions about why they should invest in basic skills education. Promising results for collaborative evaluation are evident in Massachusetts and elsewhere in the United States and Canada. In collaborative evaluations, workplace interest groups plan and implement an evaluation strategy. These evaluations provide information that is relevant to workers, program participants, management, funders, and educators.

Balanced Emphasis on Worker Skills. Another major issue is that far too much responsibility is placed on workers' basic skills and ensuing programs for improving a lagging economy, enhancing global competitiveness, improving productivity, and correcting the problems of a particular workplace. This perspective on workplace literacy affects practice when programs are unable to fulfill unrealistic expectations. The blame for failure almost always falls back on the workers. Hull (1991, p. 9) challenges popular thinking about workplace literacy when she states, "I will argue that the popular discourse of workplace literacy tends to underestimate and devalue human potential and mis-characterize literacy as a curative for problems that literacy alone cannot solve." Granted, better basic skills would help address the issues mentioned, but always in conjunction with many other strategies both at the societal level and at a particular workplace. Turk and Unda (1991) argue that the need for improved basic skills may compound problems but not cause them. They also assert that improved basic skills would assist people in tackling broader issues.

Emphasis on a model where only workers' basic skills are considered as a solution fails to recognize other employee training needs and larger organizational issues that need to be addressed. When only workers' skills are emphasized in isolation, there is the assumption that management does not need to upgrade basic skills and that organizations do not need to change their practices. A holistic approach that investigates the perspectives of employees at all levels of an organization and analyzes policies and practices is needed. This broader investigation will ensure that proper weighting is given to enhancing workers' skills and that other badly needed strategies are also considered.

Challenge to the Deficit Model: Promoting a Positive, Healthy Approach. Connected with this focus on workers' skills is the emphasis on workers' deficits and the disrespectful language that is used to describe workers' basic skills needs. Imel and Kerka (1992) found that many issues related to workplace literacy programs have to do with the dehumanizing ways workers' literacy needs are depicted. These ways of portraying workers and literacy must be challenged. Employees do not come to workplace programs as empty vessels that need to be filled. Rather they come to programs with intelligence, life experiences, knowledge, and well-developed sets of job skills.

A deficit model will curtail the success of workplace programs and impede the progress of both individuals and organizations. Not only is a model that focuses on deficiencies inaccurate, it also undermines the development of self-esteem and self-confidence, the foundation for all learning. What is needed is a model of workplace education that builds positively on the knowledge, experience, and skills of the workforce both in its approach and language. Building on this foundation can begin during the planning stages through an employee-driven committee. Needs assessments that solicit the ideas and perspectives of all interest groups in a workplace can also promote a positive approach. They can create enthusiasm and buy-in by showing employees that their opinions and experience are valued. This translates into welcome participation in employee-centered programs further down the line.

Alternative to the Quick Fix. Another current issue that ties in with a deficit approach is the belief that basic skills needs can be addressed quickly without much attention to the larger workplace context. For example, employers commonly ask for a test they can give their workers so they can identify those who need a program, run the program, and be done with basic skills. This is an outmoded approach to education that will not serve the needs of workplaces that are moving to teamwork and more employee decision making. Employers will likely not find that this approach addresses their short-term and long-term goals. Nor will the individuals who participate in the programs.

On the other hand, employers who recognize that addressing basic and other educational needs is an ongoing, evolving, and developmental process are likely to have more success in achieving their goals. Employers who realize that workers at all levels (including management) will probably need to improve their skills are likely to have more positive results.

A long-term strategy involves getting the input on educational needs from all workplace interest groups rather than giving people a test. It means developing strategies over time to address many different needs, and having the users of programs involved in program design. It includes ongoing and end-of-cycle evaluations to make sure strategies are on track and achieving what they are supposed to. Involving employees in the planning, development, and implementation of these strategies takes longer but ultimately contributes to their success. An approach that utilizes employee involvement complements the efforts of organizations moving to more employee decision making.

Workplace Development

Key principles of good practice (Folinsbee and Jurmo, 1994b) for workplace development include a focus on the basics. These principles can clearly guide and inform practice and can work to build successful workplace initiatives.

Sometimes these principles overlap. No principle should be sacrificed at the expense of another.

Holistic Approach. A holistic approach considers basic skills needs within a larger workplace framework. Within this framework basic skills are interwoven with other workplace issues. *Holistic* also refers to the whole person. A holistic approach would consider the needs of an individual not only as a worker, but also as a parent and as a citizen.

This principle is reflected in practice in several ways. First, a committee representing the perspectives of workers and management guides the planning and implementation process. Second, an organizational needs assessment (Folinsbee and Jurmo, 1994a) is conducted before any individual needs assessments. This assessment involves, among other things, a sampling of all levels of the workforce. It provides the big picture of basic skills needs and how they fit with other educational needs and workplace issues. It determines a plan of action that includes next steps, needed programs, and other complementary strategies. For example, an organizational assessment might show that there is a need for a clear language policy. A committee might be formed to develop this policy, to rewrite key workplace documents, and to organize clear writing workshops. It might also show there is a need to consider a literacy task analysis for positions that are changing, or that better communication channels must be developed.

An organizational needs assessment at a British Columbia sawmill identified relationship and communication issues with respect to the culturally and racially diverse workforce. These issues were addressed in the implementation phase along with workplace programs to improve basic skills. As a result of this integrated effort to deal with pressing needs around diversity, more people felt safe to get involved in the workplace education programs. Collaborative evaluation (Jurmo and Folinsbee, 1994; Sperazi and Jurmo, 1994) includes workers, management, and others in the planning and implementation phases. It considers needed program improvements and expected and unexpected outcomes in an integrated way with the organizational needs assessment and program development.

Promising practices also integrate basic skills with actual problem-solving situations identified by program participants that relate to both their work and their home lives. Participants enhance their basic skills while they are actually finding solutions to real workplace problems. A good example of this practice can be found in New York State's federally funded workplace literacy project.

A holistic approach ensures that basic skills are connected to other key workplace issues. It also ensures that workplace education programs are not expected to shoulder too much of the responsibility for problems they cannot solve, and helps identify strategies to address some of these other issues. This approach builds transferable skills that benefit organizations in their need for a flexible, well-rounded workforce but also benefits individuals at work and at home.

Inclusion and Collaboration. This means involving both workers and managers in the planning and implementation of workplace initiatives. It means giving all interest groups in the workplace a voice. For example, in a diverse workplace it is essential to have representatives from key groups on your planning committee. It is also necessary to have a representative sampling of these groups in the organizational needs assessment and evaluation.

Inclusion and collaboration can also be reflected at the program level. For example, barriers that might prevent certain employees from participating in programs need to be addressed. If a program is held at the end of the day shift, employees with responsibility for children and those from other shifts may not be able to attend. It is important to ensure that programs are welcoming to all and sensitive to workforce diversity. This means using materials and approaches to learning that are inclusive.

The most successful programs are those in which workers are involved in developing and designing programs (Sarmiento and Kay, 1990). Inclusion and collaboration are crucial because they build buy-in and ownership from all groups at the workplace. When all voices are heard, there is a better chance that the needs of all interest groups will be served and programs will be successful for both individuals and organizations.

Integration for Long-Term Commitment. Workplace basic skills programs need to be part of a well-rounded training and development strategy rather than something that is separate. Programs and strategies need to be tailored to corporate and union short and long-term goals. A financial commitment to include basic skills as part of an overall strategy needs to be made. Strategies to address basic skills need to be incorporated into other training and education. For example, instructors should cater to many different learning styles and be cognizant of whether the print materials they are using are necessary, are written in clear language, and are tailored to the audience. In addition, they can use strategies to help their participants enhance their reading and writing skills.

One Ontario-based manufacturing firm found from an organizational needs assessment that it needed to develop a training and education system that would integrate basic skills. For example, in designing new, job-specific courses, it would be important to canvass the end-users of the program. Basic skills needs of future participants would need to be considered in the design of the course. The organizational needs assessment showed that it is important to conduct an individual needs assessment for participants for all courses. Part of the individual needs assessment would always include a basic skills component. In-house instructors in this company needed some awareness and skills to address basic skills needs in their courses.

Integration of basic skills at both the macro and micro levels can help ensure a long-term commitment to workplace education. This long-term commitment will contribute to the achievement of short- and long-term company goals.

Positive, Respectful Approach. An approach that is respectful of the skills, abilities, and knowledge that people bring to learning is paramount. Positive language that emphasizes building on what people know is crucial. For example, this principle is reflected in practice in employee-driven workplace committees, organizational needs assessments, collaborative approaches to evaluation, and participant-centered programs. A positive approach asserts that learning is ongoing and that everyone in an organization can improve his or her skills, even the basics. For example, if workers see their managers improving their basic skills, they are more likely to feel secure doing the same.

Workplace initiatives that are respectful avoid terms that suggest deficiencies and disease and warlike metaphors. Instead, they talk about opportunities for employee development. For example, one program committee called its initiative LIFT, Learning Initiatives for Tomorrow. Another committee developed a logo that not only reflected positive learning but also captured the company culture.

Future Directions

In order to ensure the sustainability of workplace basic skills education and promotion of effective practice, we must advocate for strong leadership from policymakers at the state, provincial, and federal levels. We must also continue to address and debunk popular stereotypes about workers and basic skills. We need to build more evidence and support for basic skills initiatives. A collaborative approach to evaluation is one promising practice that can provide us with feedback on what we are achieving and where we need to improve. In addition, there is a need to promote and conduct more ethnographic research in workplaces that are attempting to follow these principles to see the effect that initiatives have on organizations as well as on the lives of individuals.

There are many exemplary programs that reflect the principles and practices outlined in this chapter. However, I believe there is a need to build on the principles outlined here. We must continue to enrich and enhance our practice at every stage of the planning and implementation stage as an ongoing endeavor.

References

Askov, E. N., and Alderman, B. "Understanding the History and Definitions of Workplace Literacy." In M. C. Taylor, G. R. Lewe, and J. A. Draper (eds.), *Basic Skills for the Workplace*. Toronto: Culture Concepts Inc., 1991.

Canadian Labour Market and Productivity Centre. *National Training Survey*. Ottawa: Canadian Labour Market and Productivity Centre, 1993.

Darrah, C. N. "Workplace Skills in Context." Unpublished manuscript, 1991.

Doran, J. *The Basic Skills Training Survey*. Toronto: Canadian Grocery Producers Joint Human Resources Committee, 1995.

Folinsbee, S. *Workplace Literacy and Basics Skills*. Ottawa, Canada: National Literacy Secretariat, 1995.

Folinsbee, S., and Jurmo, P. *Collaborative Needs Assessment: A Handbook for Workplace Development Planners*. Toronto: ABC Canada, 1994a.

Folinsbee, S., and Jurmo, P. *Collaborative Workplace Development: An Overview*. Toronto: ABC Canada, 1994b.

Gowen, S. G. *The Politics of Workplace Literacy: A Case Study*. New York: Teachers College Press, 1992.

Hull, G. *Hearing Other Voices: A Critical Assessment of Popular Views of Literacy and Work.* Berkeley: National Center for Research in Vocational Education, University of California, 1991.

Imel, S., and Kerka, S. *Workplace Literacy: A Guide to the Literature and Resources.* Columbus: ERIC Clearinghouse on Adult, Career, and Vocational Education, Center on Education and Training for Employment, College of Education, Ohio State University, 1992.

Jurmo, P. *Workplace Education: Stakeholders' Expectations, Practitioners' Responses, and the Role Evaluation Might Play.* Washington, D.C.: National Institute for Literacy, 1994.

Jurmo, P., and Folinsbee, S. *Collaborative Evaluation: A Handbook for Workplace Development Planners.* Toronto: ABC Canada, 1994.

National Literacy Secretariat. *Policy Conversation on Workplace/Workforce Literacy: A Report.* Ottawa, Canada: National Literacy Secretariat, 1995.

Sarmiento, A. R., and Kay, A. *Worker-Centered Learning: A Union Guide to Workplace Literacy.* Washington, D.C.: AFL-CIO Human Resources Development Institute, 1990.

Shultz, K. *Training for Basic Skills or Educating Workers? Changing Conceptions of Workplace Education Programs.* Berkeley: National Center for Research in Vocational Education, University of California, 1992.

Sperazi, L., and Jurmo, P. *Team Evaluation: A Guide to Workplace Education Programs.* Washington, D.C.: National Institute for Literacy, 1994.

Stein, S. G. " Workplace Literacy and the Transformation of the American Workplace: A Model for Effective Practice." Unpublished manuscript, 1990.

Turk, J., and Unda, J. "So We Can Make Our Voices Heard: The Ontario Federation of Labour's BEST Project on Worker Literacy." In M. C. Taylor, G. R. Lewe, and J. A Draper (eds.), *Basic Skills for the Workplace.* Toronto: Culture Concepts Inc., 1991.

U.S. Department of Education. *Workplace Literacy: Reshaping the American Workforce.* Washington, D.C.: U.S. Department of Education, Office of Vocational and Adult Education, Division of Adult Education and Literacy, 1992.

U.S. Department of Labor and U.S. Department of Education. *The Bottom Line: Basic Skills in the Workplace.* Washington, D.C.: U.S. Department of Labor and U.S. Department of Education, 1988.

Young, C. D. *Asking New Questions: Assessment for Workplace Literacy.* Albany: Civil Service Employees Association Inc. and New York State Governor's Office of Employee Relations, 1994.

SUE WAUGH FOLINSBEE is director of workplace education for ABC Canada.

Information technologies are important tools that augment individual, team, and organizational learning. Recent developments will permit information technologies to enhance the relationship between work and learning.

Information Technologies and Workplace Learning

Gene L. Roth

Several writers have suggested that technological developments will drastically alter the way we think about teaching, learning, and working. Emerging technological systems are expected to alter traditional constraints involved in work and learning, such as time, place, safety, language, and culture. Information technologies, like other forms of technology, have a history of permeating our ways of being before we fully understand their consequences. For example, several decades ago lighted overhead projection was used in bowling alleys as a screen display for bowling scores. The technological offspring of those early units have migrated into classrooms and training centers as overhead projectors. These tools are now considered a staple by trainers who want to meet the needs of visual learners.

This chapter examines themes and issues regarding information technologies and workplace learning. A few emerging information technologies will be discussed in terms of workplace learning. Issues regarding the integration of technology into an organization's culture will be examined. Topics pertaining to adult educators and their needs will be examined. Caveats regarding information technologies and learning in the workplace will be discussed. A glimpse of workplace learning in the future will be explored. Concluding thoughts will be offered regarding researchable issues for information technologies and workplace learning.

Emerging Information Technologies

In this brief chapter it is impossible to highlight the many information technologies used for workplace learning. Several technologies have infiltrated the processes in which we work, teach, and learn. In many ways the technologies have become transparent to us. We tend to take many of them for granted. The automatic teller machine (ATM) is a good example. We do not think of the complex nature of the multiple transactions that take place across banks when we insert an ATM card; we simply expect to get our money quickly and effortlessly.

The same type of transparency is sought from information technologies used for teaching and learning. The technology should be insignificant to the learner. The center of attention should be the quality of learning. The technology should merely serve as a tool that is helping a person in a learning situation.

Information technology is a term that encompasses a variety of hardware and software configurations, including computer-based instruction systems, distance learning technologies, and integrated learning systems. This section highlights two types of information technologies that have unique capabilities for enhancing workplace learning: virtual reality (VR) and the Internet.

Virtual Reality. Futuristic accounts describing virtual reality and its potential for creative applications are common. What is virtual reality and what can we reasonably expect from it as an aid to workplace learning? Several definitions of virtual reality appear in the literature. Hedberg and Alexander (1994) cite the following definitions and their sources:

VR is a computer-generated, multidimensional, inclusive environment that can be accepted by the participant as cognitively valid.

Objects, attributes, and relationships set in natural or surreal contexts.

VR becomes a way of sensing, feeling, and thinking. The computer controls sensation by controlling the input to the senses, altering experience, emotion, and ultimately thought.

Most observers consider virtual reality to be in rudimentary stages of development. However, the potential of this technology for teaching and learning in the workplace appears to be great. It provides workers simulated practice that can help them move from the realm of novice to that of expert worker. Workers can try out practices and procedures in "virtual" work situations. Virtual reality appears to have many positive attributes as a learning medium (Hedberg and Alexander, 1994):

There is an intuitive aspect of the virtual world because learners are interacting with objects and tools in authentic ways.

The virtual world can be programmed to provide a wide variety of practice experiences, from the simple to the complex.

Virtual objects can possess a wide range of characteristics, from abstract to realistic; a very concrete experience may be designed for an abstract concept.

Learners can practice a routine repeatedly, gaining confidence and skill from the repetitive sessions and understanding outcomes as variables are manipulated.

The system can automate procedures that are mastered by learners, allowing them to focus on new learning or viewing large parts of worker knowledge.

Virtual reality allows workplace learning for complex tasks in a simulated setting. The real learning environment or situation might be unavailable to the learner because of cost, time, safety, or other factors. Industries associated with transportation, energy, and manufacturing are currently experimenting with or using applications of virtual reality.

Because virtual reality is an emerging technology that does not have an established history as an information technology, there are many unanswered questions regarding its effectiveness and efficiency as a learning tool. Hedberg and Alexander (1994) cited the following questions: What is the relationship between learning with peers and applications of virtual reality? How does the user make sense of stories, conversations, and multiple viewpoints that are associated with communities of practice? How does learning take place in a "virtual community of practice?"

These questions suggest that maximal effectiveness with virtual reality will be achieved if the learning applications are realistic and authentic. Such learning scenarios include learning with and from peers. If virtual reality is to be used successfully as a workplace learning tool, its programming should not isolate problems and learning tasks from the worker's context. The "virtual community of practice" should replicate the ill-structured problems associated with complex work environments.

Internet. An emerging information technology that has recently gained ample attention is the Internet. It is often called the Information Superhighway, but most novice users probably view it more as a "lost at sea" experience. Early adapters of this technology struggled with the immense amount of information that confronted them. They found few guideposts available that could help them find their ways along this vast landscape of information. Navigational tools now make the search for information easier. The World Wide Web is operated by computer programs that are designed to link data stored in computers connected to the Internet (Rubin, 1994). With the emergence of software such as Mosaic and Netscape the World Wide Web is more manageable. The complexity of the World Wide Web becomes less apparent to the user. Self-directed learning is used by most people who seek to develop skills in using the World Wide Web. Catalogs, books, and user groups help novices teach themselves to maneuver in the World Wide Web.

People use the Internet for three basic purposes: communicating with others, seeking information, and obtaining files from distant locations (Rubin, 1994). The Internet is a vast warehouse of information that is continuously growing and changing. Although learners might be intimidated by this system, the Internet and the World Wide Web are rich resources that should be accessed by workers and learners. Perhaps one of the most interesting developments with the emergence of the Internet is how people gather there to find information. The unique aspect of this evolution is how the information is found. We tend to think of the computer as a source of "official knowledge" that can be accessed through many data bases on the Internet. It is true that thousands of data bases are within our reach, but there are also thousands of special interest groups that network on the Internet. In other words, the Internet provides an electronic meeting room in which people with similar interests and concerns ask questions, voice opinions, recommend other sources, share information, and collaboratively solve problems. Hence, the Internet provides a form of collaborative learning in the workplace without boundaries of time, space, and distance. People are the sources of answers to our problems; computers merely allow us to converse with people in search of solutions around the world (Filipczak, 1994).

The Internet as a learning environment has created a new forum for workplace learning. Although it has removed many constraints of traditional workplace learning, it offers other variables that must be sorted through for the future (Max, cited in Filipczak, 1994):

The learning environment will be extremely large. The linking of information might foster a democratic explosion in the access of knowledge. Access to information will probably increase.

The learning environment will be messy. Information will no longer be viewed as something that is easily filed, stored, and located. Finding what you are looking for at any particular moment will be a challenge. Locations of information, and the information itself, will be in a state of flux.

There will be no teachers. The controllers of information will begin to disappear and public discourse will open up to anyone who can get on-line. Censors will lose their power.

What do these predictions mean for workplace learning? How much knowledge will workers be accountable for if they have unlimited access to information? These predictions may well signal the beginning of limitless, just-in-time learning for workers (Filipczak, 1994). Workers can expand their networks of colleagues around the world, and they will be able to communicate with them in a fraction of a second. Workers can join special interest groups in which chit-chat can be shallow and superfluous, or they can enter a collaborative dialogue that propels them into the depths of theory, gaining insights from people from around the globe whose world views have been shaped by a very different set of life experiences.

Interaction patterns on the Internet are different—perhaps not better or worse than face-to-face interactions, but certainly different. There is a leveling factor with communication on the Internet. In most cases, there do not seem to be elements of reputation, clout, or strength. People seem to have a sense of equality in their communication (Passmore, cited in Sorohan, 1994b). But what are the implications of this? How does it alter the quality of information transfer? Given the nuances of this new source of information, how does it affect knowledge creation by workers? Do they value these sources of information more or less than traditional sources of official knowledge?

For workers to move forward with this technology, first they must understand the characteristics and capabilities of a network. They need to refine their collaborative skills, become more proficient in their time management, and protect themselves against information overload (Sorohan, 1994a). They must understand that as worker-learners they have the capability to create knowledge of great value to the organization.

Access to the Internet by workers is another issue worth noting. How long will the Internet and other global communication channels be easily accessible by workers? Will organizations restrict access to the Internet as a method for controlling information? Some writers note that organizations are leery of electronic networks because of data security issues, confidentiality of company secrets, and control of information. Wylie (cited in Burrows, 1994) suggested the concept of "business information refineries" as a future development in information management. He posits that attempts to make information systems more user-friendly will fail unless the key issues regarding documentation, selection, and classification of information are better understood and improved.

Facilitators of Formal Learning in the Workplace

Formal, informal, and incidental learning can all occur in the workplace. Marsick and Watkins (1990) described informal learning as predominantly experiential and noninstitutional. Incidental learning was described as an unintentional by-product of another activity. Formal learning in the workplace was associated with training activities that are held in classes or on the job.

Those engaged in training and development are typically the change agents responsible for the formal learning of an organization. Trainers, instructional designers, and others perform roles in planning, delivering, and evaluating the training efforts. In small organizations, the training effort might be carried out by a one-person department. In larger organizations, hundreds of workers might be involved in training and development functions of the corporation.

What attitudes do trainers hold toward information technologies in the workplace? Are they early adapters or laggards when it comes to using information technologies? Perhaps they are similar to other educators, who are cautious about investing in new technologies. A study conducted by Spotts and Bowman (1993) examined factors influencing the use of technology by faculty at an American university. Faculty were most likely to use a technology if they were certain that it would have a positive impact on the student's learning. As a general rule, those who facilitate learning want to know how information technologies work and what their success rates are before they make commitments.

Trainers who oversee formal workplace learning settings share a common concern with other educators regarding this issue: evidence has not confirmed that applications of information technologies have increased learners' achievement. Those who facilitate learning, as a general rule, do not like to trade traditional instructional methods in which they have found success for newer methods that are unproven. Although the study conducted by Spotts and Bowman (1993) pertained to faculty in an institution of higher education, their concluding comments are relevant and adaptable to trainers. Trainers in the workplace will probably not be willing to invest time, energy, and money to learn instructional applications of new technologies without the presence of the following factors: good reasons to change from their traditional methods of fostering learning in the workplace, state-of-the-art equipment that is easily accessible, patient and supportive assistance in learning applications of the technology, sufficient time to learn and adapt, and learner acceptance of the technology.

These are issues facilitators of workplace learning must grapple with if they are to mesh what is known about adult teaching and learning with the power and capabilities of information technologies.

Informational Technologies and Organizational Culture

An organization's culture has a tremendous impact on how it adapts to the environment and succeeds in the global market. Senge (1990), Redding and Catalanello (1994), and Watkins and Marsick (1993) have stressed that organizational learning can provide a competitive edge that supports an organization's survival. Commitment to learning for individuals, teams, and the entire organization can help an organization put knowledge to work in creative and powerful ways.

Ruiz (1994) advocated that organizations must integrate information technologies into working and learning environments. He described integration as a situation in which information technologies are viewed as important parts of the objectives, processes, activities, and information management system of the learning environment. He posed the following suggestions:

Integration of technological environments should not be seen as an isolated activity. Integration should be viewed as an ongoing process that merges the strengths of technologies with knowledge gleaned from research and practice regarding learning in the workplace.

Technological change is not based simply on technical innovation. It is a cultural phenomenon, an important part of the evolution of society.

Integration of information technologies is congruent with the goals of workplace learning, especially when the goals focus on the development of the individual worker-learner.

Successful integration of information technologies depends on organizational willingness to adapt internal structures.

Continuing professional education, worker responsibility, and job satisfaction are key ingredients of the change process.

Workplace Learning: Infomating or Automating

Most people have opinions regarding technology and the workplace. Some people are early adapters of technology and cannot wait to try out advanced functions on their word processor. They see information technologies as new tools that will help them succeed in their work and learning. Others dread technological innovation and the changes it thrusts on them. Technology laggards would rather walk on hot coals than learn a new software package.

Opinions regarding the value of technology in the workplace are also quite varied. One may take either an optimistic or pessimistic view of a technology-laden workplace. However, it is not the technology itself that will make the workplace a desirable place for work and learning. Choices organizations make regarding work and power will determine whether optimistic or pessimistic scenarios evolve (Roth and Niemi, in press).

Zuboff (1988) described how two possible scenarios could emerge as the result of technological advances in the workplace. Her first scenario portrayed a drab view of a shallow, unfulfilling work environment. She described how the "smart machine" housed intelligence in the workplace and replaced humans as the source of critical judgment. Workers in organizations became more and more dependent, lethargic, and secretly cynical. She described how workers increasingly became disoriented because of lost meaning in work. Because of this focus on automation, jobs became isolated and remote.

Zuboff challenged us to envision another workplace of the future. In this scenario, computer-based actors and human actors augmented each other's capacities and they reached astonishing heights of knowledge generation. She described how organizational leaders acknowledged that advanced talents are needed to tap the strengths of intelligent technologies. A workforce was developed that exercised judgment in interactions with advanced technologies. She described how the level of abstract reasoning of workers increased; they understood the process of manipulating complex sets of data.

Both scenarios depicted by Zuboff might exist in the future. In fact, some of her projections are recognizable in current work settings. What factors might cause the emergence of one scenario over the other? Research conducted by Buchanan and Boddy in 1982 indicated that changes in the overall pattern of jobs and skills were determined indirectly by technology. A greater predictor of this pattern was management decisions regarding how work should be designed and controlled (cited in Forester, 1987). Management ideology is a significant influence on how technology is applied in the workplace. It may be used to create powerful learning environments for employees or it may be used to seclude workers from information and knowledge.

To achieve the "infomating" vision portrayed by Zuboff, both managers and workers must sacrifice their traditional narrow functional responsibilities and create new roles that mesh with the requirements of a data-rich environment. Workplace learning should be a natural segment of each worker's responsibilities. Authority lines must be drawn more from the relationship between knowledge and responsibility, as opposed to the traditional organizational pyramid (Zuboff, 1988).

The Future: Guarded Optimism

Adult educators are often leery of trends, themes, and innovations that seem destined to profit the organization rather than the individual worker. Cautious optimism is justified for applications of information technologies in the workplace.

Rather than jumping on the bandwagon with reckless abandon, like so many of our contemporaries, we should respond with reflective skepticism. Fundamental questions should be addressed regarding the meaning and impact of information technologies on workplace learning, teaching and learning transactions, and adult learners and their contexts (Wilson, 1994).

Whenever a technology is introduced, something is gained and something is lost. Invariably the technology brings with it unanticipated, incidental outcomes. Unanticipated outcomes can prove to be a greater benefit or a more severe detriment than the intention of the original intervention. Ruiz (1994, p. 17) cautioned us to think about the relationships between technological innovation and the delicate nature of culture: "All technologies are initially developed with specific instrumental goals in mind and are applied by people and organizations in the pursuit of economic advantages, convenience or mastery of nature. Owing to changes in the environment, however, they produce effects beyond those originally anticipated. Technological changes habitually give rise to previous unimaginable results that can be much more far-reaching than those originally obtained or desired. Good examples are to be found in fields such as agriculture, mechanics, energy, communications, electronics and health."

Visions of the Future

Office workers make up the majority of the workforce in the United States and their numbers are projected to increase. This is the group of workers whose lives are expected to be transformed by a technology-driven workplace. Several writers have forecast their visions of the office of the future. Bleecker (1991) projected that office workers will be surrounded by an array of intelligent information appliances. Techno-gadgets, referred to as information jukeboxes, will handle the chores of today's fax machines, photocopiers, printers, and monitors. Bleecker expects these integrated systems to possess powerful abilities to store, retrieve, tailor, and disseminate information. Software packages will automatically recognize, collect, and analyze information that is vital to the strategic learning efforts of an organization. Perhaps one of the most important aspects of this electronic landscape is the linking of these integrated systems (Bleecker, 1991). Workplace learning will take place via links to global information resources, worldwide electronic vendors offering a variety of services, peer workers, and systems of artificial intelligence (Roth and Niemi, in press). All of these components will contribute to learning by individuals, teams, and organizations. Organizations with the most effective means of exploiting new knowledge will be the dominant forces in the next century (Burrows, 1994).

The relationship between information technologies and workplace learning is complex. Information technologies may be viewed as mental prostheses that, if used appropriately, can help people become more effective as learners in the workplace. Carr (1992) chose the term *performance support system* to describe electronic systems that use computers and associated technology for augmenting individual learning. He described four applications of performance support systems in future work settings: the librarian, helping the performer find and use information quickly and accurately; the advisor, providing guidance and expert advice to the performer; the instructor, providing the performer with on-demand training about specific points; and the dofer (a term coined by Anthony Putman), who does as much of the routine work of the job as possible, letting the performer concentrate on more important tasks.

Thach and Woodman (1994) examined organizational change and information technology. They identified four categories of information technologies that were likely to affect organizations in the upcoming decades:

Individual work support. Thach and Woodman expect the use of high-bandwidth portable computers that will be able "to connect to any computer network around the world, at any time and any place, through an international, wireless, wide-band communication network" (p. 35). Thus, very mobile workers will be able to stay in contact with people, data bases, and organizations. Thach and Woodman state that "knowbots" will be housed inside these computers and function as personal secretaries. The knowbot will be advanced computer technology that will make judgments about types and quality of information that passes through the computer.

Group work support. Technology that helps groups or teams function more effectively is known as groupware. Groupware allows members to display their decisions regarding group problems; the computer tabulates the data quickly. Several forms of groupware are currently available, with the next generation of groupware moving toward integration with virtual reality. Groups of workers will collaborate on product design and computerized simulations will allow them to sample new products and experiences throughout developmental stages (Thach and Woodman, 1994).

Advanced organizational automation. New technologies will emerge that increase the efficiency of organizations. Thach and Woodman cite examples such as electronic data interchanges that link manufacturing and inventory functions, automated customer-response systems that move people away from direct contact with customers, and virtual reality sales that allow customers to sample realistic simulations of products, services, and experiences.

Enhanced global communications. Voice mail, electronic mail, and audio and video conferencing are communication strategies currently used by organizations to communicate at a distance. Thach and Woodman report that speech language translators are still in rudimentary forms but they show great potential for the future. These devices will be able to provide instantaneous language translations for organizations conducting international business transactions. Another technology that they noted is telepresence. This technology will allow people to project their images into meeting rooms that might be located on the other side of the globe. The image will be able to talk, see, hear, and move as though it were actually in the room (Thach and Woodman, 1994). This technology will have a significant impact on several types of global negotiations.

Information Technologies and Workplace Learning: Identifying Researchable Issues

"The future isn't what it used to be" is an expression that can aptly be used to describe workplace learning. No longer viewed as a serendipitous side effect of work, workplace learning is now viewed as the means by which most people acquire their greatest amount of job-related knowledge and skill that will take them forward in their careers.

Advances in technology are making us rethink the processes of workplace learning. We are considering the attributes of emerging information technologies and examining how their strengths might enhance the quality of learning in the workplace. Given the attributes of these systems and what we know about workplace learning, how do we map out areas of research? Gleaned from the sources cited in this chapter, the following questions draw attention to several researchable issues:

In what ways can technologies be used to increase the depth, breadth, and speed of workplace learning?

How can information technologies be integrated with or contribute to experiential learning, action learning, learning how to learn, and other components or aspects of workplace learning?

What applications of information technologies are best suited for individual, team, or organizational learning?

How will workers manage time, space, and information when traditional constraints for these entities have been removed or significantly altered?

How will workers make meaning from sources of information that are from global electronic sources or virtual reality?

How will the learning culture of an organization be altered when workers are seeking answers to questions not from the traditional pyramid structure of an organization but from vast electronic networks of peer workers, vendors, data bases, and artificial intelligence systems?

What new knowledge base will emerge regarding collaborative learning from a distance?

What new insights will emerge in the area of learning how to learn, as workers struggle to learn with information technologies that serve as advisors, instructors, librarians, and "dofers"?

Information technologies have already made a significant impact on the way organizations stay in business (Thach and Woodman, 1994). The manner in which individuals, teams, and organizations learn is a key for organizational survival (Senge, 1990, Redding and Catalanello, 1994). The relationship between workplace learning and information technologies will continue to grow in importance as organizations strive to keep their learning processes crisp and responsive.

References

Bleecker, S. "The Information Age Office." *The Futurist,* 1991, *23* (1), 18–20.

Burrows, B. "The Power of Information: Developing the Knowledge-Based Organization." *International Journal of Strategic Planning,* 1994, *27* (1), 142–152.

Carr, C. "PSS! Help When You Need It." *Training and Development,* 1992, *46* (6), 31–38.

Filipczak, B. "Trainers on the Net." *Training and Development,* 1994, *31* (12), 42–51.

Forester, T. *High-Tech Society.* Cambridge, Mass.: MIT Press, 1987.

Gordon, J. "Work Teams: How Far Have They Come?" *Training,* Oct. 1992, pp. 59–64.

Hedberg, J., and Alexander, S. "Virtual Reality in Education: Defining Researchable Issues." *Educational Media International,* 1994, *31* (4), 214–220.

Marsick, V., and Watkins, K. *Informal and Incidental Learning in the Workplace.* London: Routledge, 1990.

Redding, J. C., and Catalanello, R. F. *Strategic Readiness: The Making of the Learning Organization.* San Francisco: Jossey-Bass, 1994.

Roth, G., and Niemi, J. "Information Technologies and the Learning Organization." *International Journal of Lifelong Education,* in press.

Rubin, B. "The Internet: Where Few Trainers Have Gone Before." *Training and Development,* 1994, *48* (8), 25–30.

Ruiz, F. "The Integration of the New Technological Environments in Education." *Educational Media International,* 1994, *31* (1), 16–24.

Senge, P. *The Fifth Discipline: The Art and Practice of the Learning Organization.* New York: Doubleday, 1990.

Sorohan, E. "The Attractions of the Internet." *Training and Development Journal,* 1994a, *48* (8), 31–37.

Sorohan, E. "Trainers Network on the Net." *Training and Development Journal,* 1994b, *48* (8), 35–37.

Spotts, T., and Bowman, M. "Increasing Faculty Use of Instructional Technology: Barriers and Incentives." *Educational Media International,* 1993, *30* (4), 199–204.

Thach, L., and Woodman, R. "Organizational Change and Information Technology: Managing on the Edge of Cyberspace." *Organizational Dynamics,* Summer 1994, pp. 30–46.

Watkins, K. "Business and Industry." In S. B. Merriam and P. M. Cunningham (eds.), *Handbook of Adult and Continuing Education.* San Francisco: Jossey-Bass, 1989.

Watkins, K. E., and Marsick, V. J. *Sculpting the Learning Organization: Lessons in the Art and Science of Systematic Change.* San Francisco: Jossey-Bass, 1993.

Wellins, R. S. "Building a Self-Directed Work Team." *Training and Development Journal,* 1992, *46* (12), 24–28.

Wilson, B. "Technology and Higher Education: In Search of Progress in Human Learning." *Educational Record,* 1994, *75* (3), 9–16.

Zuboff, S. *In the Age of the Smart Machine.* New York: Basic Books, 1988.

GENE L. ROTH is director of the Office of Human Resource Development and Workforce Preparation and is an associate professor of adult and continuing education at Northern Illinois University.

To meet the competitive challenges of the years ahead, workplace educators must continue to provide innovative educational solutions to business problems.

Future Directions in Workplace Learning

W. Franklin Spikes

The role of education in the workplace of the late 1990s is one of growing importance and influence. The reengineered, downsized workforce is more dependent than ever on the development of new, transferable skill sets. Employees will be faced with different types of organizations in which managerial hierarchies become flatter, teams and work groups dominate, and new patterns of work such as job sharing, home-based work sites, and variable work hours become the norm rather than the exception to the norm. These changes, along with those brought by the value differences of an increasingly diverse and multiple-generation workforce, clearly will cause workplace educators to continually examine how they can best meet the unique demands of tomorrow's competitive business environment. Although forecasting the future is at best an inexact science, reason and past practice seem to indicate that three areas merit attention by tomorrow's workplace educator. These are employee development and learning, organization change and policy development, and use of resources.

Employee Development

The workforce of the twenty-first century will be markedly different in composition from its current counterpart. More women, people of color, non-native English speakers, older workers, and members of multiple generations will be present in the workforce. Workplace educators of the future must look beyond the concept of training as the basis and primary focus for their work. Instead, the more broad concept of employee development must be embraced as the cornerstone on which workplace education programs of the next decade should be built. Workplace educators who adopt an employee development focus will naturally look to address a wide range of human performance-related issues. Among these issues should be the development of ongoing career development systems that encourage employees to develop transferable skill sets appropriate to a variety of jobs. More particularly, workplace learning initiatives must begin to focus on broad-based skill-development and career-planning initiatives that will prepare people to make the increasingly numerous job and career transitions that will be a routine element in the lives of future workers.

In addition to this emphasis, future workplace learning programs must give special attention to addressing the social, cultural, and value-based issues brought to the workplace by an increasingly pluralistic group of workers. The workforce of the future will find that it is no longer sufficient to address race, gender, and intergenerational value matters on an intermittent basis as a response to a litigious or potentially litigious situation. Separatism cannot exist in the workforce of tomorrow. As the movement toward self-directed, team-oriented employee groups escalates and becomes the norm, so should the initiatives of workplace educators increase with regard to building cohesive work units composed of people of multiple generations, races, genders, and life-style orientations.

Last, with respect to the focus on employee development concerns, tomorrow's workplace educator must look for expanded, innovative ways to develop educational programs built on a solid research base of knowledge about adult learning. Instruction methodologies must be developed that help employees integrate and apply the vast amount of information that will be needed in their jobs in the years ahead. Future workplace learning initiatives must be tied to the immediacy of application needed by workers in tomorrow's just-in-time organizations. Likewise, instructional mechanisms must be built to help workers learn through individualization and self-directed learning. Just-in-time learning, or learning what is needed in a way that is immediately applicable to employees' work roles and allows them to learn in a way that takes maximum advantage of their unique learning styles and preferences, must become the basis for workplace learning programs in the next decade.

Organizational Change

Tomorrow's organizations will take on a shape and character that are substantially different from those of their current counterparts. Workplace learning initiatives will also change. However, it is the latter that must play a key role in the transformation of the former. Workplace educators of the future must expand their role in the process of organizational transformation. Learning must be seen as a primary goal of an increasingly broad-based group of tomorrow's globally competitive firms. In doing so, workplace learning professionals must be positioned in the organization in a way that reflects their importance for business growth and development. Examination of core business issues with respect to growth, expansion, downsizing, or reengineering must always include an analysis of the relationships of learning to change and learning to employee growth and development. As people and organizations change, workplace educators must drive the process. They must become the advocates for the human performance factors present in the change process. That must lead the growth of tomorrow's organizational change process in a way that uses the potential of all employees to better their work environment and enhance the productivity and profitability of their employer.

Policy Development and Use of Resources

The third area to which workplace educators must address their attention in the years ahead is policy development and resource use. Government agencies concerned with employment and employability issues must develop and put in place nationwide educational and economic development policies that encourage the implementation and sustenance of workplace learning initiatives. Employees must be encouraged to put in place a variety of learning-related initiatives that will allow them to become more knowledgeable, thus allowing their organizations to attain greater economic competitiveness. Employees must be given opportunities to learn and be rewarded for doing so. The development of national initiatives of workforce development described earlier in this volume can no longer wait. Leadership at the state and federal level must be encouraged to view advancing the state of workplace learning initiatives as a key public policy priority to achieve in the immediate future. Likewise, the public and private sectors must join together in a way that makes more effective use of limited resources in a time of escalating fiscal demands for both government and business. Joint workplace learning partnerships must expand. Public schools, unions, and government agencies must work together if the demands of tomorrow's workplace are to effectively be met.

Ultimately, and beyond the employee, organizational, and policy development concerns described above, the future and success of workplace learning initiatives depend on our willingness as a society to shed the educational practices of the past and transform ourselves and our thinking in a way that maximizes the value we place on learning, change, and growth throughout the working lives of our citizens.

W. FRANKLIN SPIKES is professor, Department of Foundations and Adult Education, Kansas State University.

INDEX

Academy of Human Resource Development, 10

Academy of Management, 10

Adult Education Act, 66

Adult education, graduate study in, 57–58

Aid for Families with Dependent Children (AFDC), 22

Alderman, B., 65

Alexander, S., 76, 77

Allen, C. R., 5

American Association for Adult and Continuing Education (AAACE), 48

American College Testing Proficiency Examination Program, 50

American College Testing Service, 55

American Council on Education (ACE): awarding of credit recommendations by, 44–45; background of, 41; Center for Adult Learning and Educational Credentials (CALEC), 40–41, 44, 50; courses evaluated by, 41; Credit by Examination Program, 43; evaluation process, 41–42; and evaluation of workplace learning, 42–44; and experiential learning, 48; function of, 40; Government Affairs office, 41; and military training, evaluation of, 49; and nontraditional learning, 44–45; Office of International Initiatives, 41; Office of Leadership Development, 41; Office of Minority Affairs, 41; Office of Policy Analysis and Research, 41; Program on Noncollegiate Sponsored Instruction (PONSI), 49, 51, 52; publication of findings by, 44; Registry of Credit Recommendations, 44

American Society for Training and Development (ASTD), 6, 8, 10

American Society of Training Directors, 6. See also American Society for Training and Development (ASTD)

Apprenticeships, 22

Arthur Andersen Consulting, 7, 12

Askov, E. N., 65

Aslanian, C. B., 51

Association for Continuing Higher Education (ACHE), 48

Automation of workplace learning, 80–81

Ball, C., 40

Basic skills: balanced emphasis on, 68; in Canada, 65, 66, 67, 70, 71; collaborative approach to, 63, 67, 70; critical issues, 67–69; and deficit model, 68–69; definitions of, 64–65; development of, 63; versus entry-level skills, 65; evaluations of programs for, 68; functional context approach, 66; future of, 72; history of, 65–66; investment in, 67; needs of workers, 63; participatory approach to, 67; programs, 63; trends in, 66–67; and workplace development, 65; versus workplace education, 65

Bleecker, S., 82

Bowman, M., 79

Brickell, H. M., 51

Brown, J., 13

Burrows, B., 79, 82

Canton, Ohio v. Harris, 12

Career Education Act, 24–25

Carnegie Commission, 47

Carnevale, A. P., 1, 2, 7, 8, 9, 28, 47, 51, 55

Carnevale, E. S., 1, 2, 55

Carr, C., 82–83

Catalanello, R. F., 80, 84

Center for Adult Learning and Educational Credentials (CALEC), 40–41, 44, 50

Charter Oak College, 48

Civilian Conservation Corps (CCC), 5, 22

"Coach-to-principal" approach, 56–57

Coalition of Adult Education Organizations (CAEO), 48

College Board, 48, 50, 52

College-Level Examination Program (CLEP), 49, 50

Commission of Professors of Adult Education, 57

Commission on the Skills of the American Workforce, 29

Commission on Technology and the American Economy, 27

Company sponsored training, 39. See also Workplace learning

Comprehensive Employment and Training Act (CETA), 5, 24, 25, 26

ORDERING INFORMATION

NEW DIRECTIONS FOR ADULT AND CONTINUING EDUCATION is a series of paperback books that explores issues of common interest to instructors, administrators, counselors, and policy makers in a broad range of adult and continuing education settings—such as colleges and universities, extension programs, businesses, the military, prisons, libraries, and museums. Books in the series are published quarterly in Spring, Summer, Fall, and Winter and are available for purchase by subscription and individually.

SUBSCRIPTIONS for 1995 cost $48.00 for individuals (a savings of 36 percent over single-copy prices) and $64.00 for institutions, agencies, and libraries. Standing orders are accepted. New York residents, add local sales tax for subscriptions. (For subscriptions outside the United States, add $7.00 for shipping via surface mail or $25.00 for air mail. Orders *must be prepaid* in U.S. dollars by check drawn on a U.S. bank or charged to VISA, MasterCard, or American Express.)

SINGLE COPIES cost $19.00 plus shipping (see below) when payment accompanies order. California, New Jersey, New York, and Washington, D.C., residents please include appropriate sales tax. Canadian residents add GST and any local taxes. Billed orders will be charged shipping and handling. No billed shipments to post office boxes. (Orders from outside the United States *must be prepaid* in U.S. dollars by check drawn on a U.S. bank or charged to VISA, MasterCard, or American Express.)

SHIPPING (SINGLE COPIES ONLY): one issue, add $5.00; two issues, add $6.00; three issues, add $7.00; four to five issues, add $8.00; six to seven issues, add $9.00; eight or more issues, add $12.00.

DISCOUNTS FOR QUANTITY ORDERS are available. Please write to the address below for information.

ALL ORDERS must include either the name of an individual or an official purchase order number. Please submit your order as follows:
Subscriptions: specify series and year subscription is to begin
Single copies: include individual title code (such as ACE 59)

MAIL ALL ORDERS TO:
Jossey-Bass Publishers
350 Sansome Street
San Francisco, California 94104-1342

FOR SUBSCRIPTION SALES OUTSIDE OF THE UNITED STATES, contact any international subscription agency or Jossey-Bass directly.

OTHER TITLES AVAILABLE IN THE
NEW DIRECTIONS FOR ADULT AND CONTINUING EDUCATION SERIES
Ralph G. Brockett, Susan Imel, Editors-in-Chief
Alan B. Knox, Consulting Editor